I0224827

Spiritual Lights in Benighted Times

Fifteen Christian Outliers

HARRY OLDMEADOW

Spiritual Lights in Benighted Times

Fifteen Christian Outliers

☩

𝕏 Angelico Press

Originally published by Carbarita Press
(Bendigo, Australia) in 2022 as *Against the Tide:
Sketches of Modern Christian Thinkers*
First US edition, Angelico Press 2025
© Angelico Press 2025

All rights reserved

No part of this book may be reproduced or transmitted,
in any form or by any means, without permission.

For information, address:
Angelico Press
169 Monitor St.
Brooklyn, NY 11222
angelicopress.com

979-8-89280-124-9 (pbk)
979-8-89280-125-6 (cloth)

Cover design: Michael Schrauzer

CONTENTS

For Steve and Paul

companions on the way

Introduction

gainst the Tide brings together some modern Christian thinkers—philosophers, theologians, monks and mystics, novelists among them—who have wrestled with some of the most urgent issues of our times. As our title suggests, being a serious Christian in the modern world is necessarily to be out of tune with the prevailing *Zeitgeist*, at odds with the secular-materialist-humanist worldview that now holds sway in most parts of the world. Most of these thinkers found cause for deep alarm in this state of affairs. I count myself fortunate to have met three of my subjects in person (Bede Griffiths, Huston Smith, James Cowan), but all have enriched my life. I hope these sketches, a labor of love, go some little distance towards repaying the debt. In any event, each has something important to say to our troubled times. The possible inclusions were many. I have had to omit some of the usual suspects—C. S. Lewis and T. S. Eliot, to name a couple—not because they are less important, but because they have already been so much written about. In any case, one has to draw the line somewhere. There were also other less well-known Christian thinkers who at one time or another loomed large in my inner life but who have not found their way into the present volume; Nikos Kazantzakis, for instance. Perhaps next time?

Any objective attempt at a fair cross-section of contemporary Christian thought would include thinkers from the "Third World," indigenous believers, and theologians working at the interface of the tradition and contemporary theoretical/political movements such as feminism, post-colonialism, and eco-philosophy, all absent in this avowedly subjective project. Nonetheless, I hope the selection reflects some of the diversity in this field.

Most of these small essays are neither biographies nor overviews. They are rather, mainly, discursive and informal pieces that pursue an isolated theme or a single aspect of the thinking of the person in question. My intentions are neither scholarly nor hagiographical.

None of these figures were saints, though some undoubtedly had saintly qualities. T. S. Eliot somewhere opined that we should judge societies not by their GDP or their tally of Olympic medals, but by the number of saints they produced. The twentieth century record, in the West at least, is not reassuring. Celebrities, not saints, are the order of the day.

With one exception all of the featured thinkers spent most of their lives in the twentieth century. This was one of the principles of selection. I'm interested in Christian critiques of modernity, a theme that comes into sharper focus if our purview is restricted to this period. Other recurrent themes include the "problem" of religious pluralism, the timeless relevance of the perennial philosophy, the place of mysticism in religious life, and the "lessons of the nomads." The exclusion of all pre-twentieth-century figures is waived for one exception, Fyodor Dostoevsky (1821–1881). Unlike most of his contemporaries, the Russian novelist foresaw with chilling prescience many of the developments that would give the twentieth century its peculiar character. In this respect he anticipates many of the issues that have disturbed Christian thinkers in more recent times. Dostoevsky was also one of the most profound religious thinkers of the modern era. He seemed like a good starting point for the somewhat unruly compilation that follows; he would no doubt be surprised by some of his bed-fellows in the present volume. The entries are organized chronologically by birth dates. Following Plato's advice that rules are for the obedience of the foolish and the guidance of the wise, I have violated the chronology by situating Solzhenitsyn last, thus achieving a kind of symmetry by starting and finishing with two great Russian writers, fervent disciples of the Galilean and fierce critics of modernity both.

The book is addressed to anyone with an interest in "Christian thought" in any of its variegated and sometimes wildly divergent expressions. As *Against the Tide* is not, in the first place, addressed to scholars, I have dispensed with many of the protocols and impedimenta of academic writing. Readers wishing to track down undocumented quotes and sources will find them easily enough on the web. Digital technology, full of sinister possibilities, does, after all, have *some* uses.

Introduction

I was encouraged and supported in this project by Brian Coman, Steve Maber, Rose Mazza, Peter Thompson, and Paul Weeks. I thank them all.

BENDIGO
December 2021

Fyodor Michailovich Dostoevsky

1821–1881

Christian Themes in the Great Novels

There is only one thing I dread:
not to be worthy of my sufferings.[1]

n 1849 the Tsarist police in St Petersburg were rounding up political suspects. Members of the Petrashevsky Circle, a literary group of sorts, were arrested for circulating books critical of the Tsarist regime. One of those apprehended and sentenced to death was Fyodor Mikhailovich Dostoevsky, military engineer, journalist, translator, emerging novelist and, on the face of it, a political dissident.[2] Dostoevsky was actually lined up before a mock firing squad (all too real for him!), but given a staged last-minute reprieve. He gives us a graphic account of what he believed were the last few minutes of his life in *The Idiot*. The sentence was commuted, and Dostoevsky sent into a ten-year exile in Siberia. He spent four years in a squalid hard labor prison camp, vividly depicted in *The House of the Dead*, followed by six years of compulsory military service. At the time of his arrest Dostoevsky's intellectual life was largely shaped by his wide reading of Western authors including Cervantes, Shakespeare, Dickens, Goethe and Schiller, and by the works of his compatriots Pushkin and Gogol. For a short while he was a participant in the utopian socialist Betekov Circle, another of St Peterburg's burgeoning discussion groups, this one focused on the writings of such figures as Fourier, Proudhon, and Saint-Simon. However, Dostoevsky didn't fit comfortably into any of the Westward-looking anti-Tsarist groups, one of the stumbling blocks being his growing commitment to Orthodox Christianity, which only matured during his Siberian exile. During his four years in the labor camp, prisoners were allowed to read only one book, the *New Testament*. Some of Dostoevsky's biographers have made much of this in explaining Dostoevsky's apparent transformation from radical socialist to deeply conservative Slavophile, defender of Orthodoxy and Tsardom, and ferocious critic of all Western European ideologies. The fact is that from a young age he had been raised in a religious family, had been a dedicated reader of the Scriptures, and had never actually repudiated the Christian faith despite his early flirtation with radical secular ideologies. Nonetheless, it is also true that it was only his later immersion, in Siberia, in the mystical Gospel of St John, that fully convinced him of the divinity of Christ.[3]

Released from exile, Dostoevsky returned to St Petersburg in

1859. Over the next twenty years he published some of the most remarkable works in world literature, including *Crime and Punishment*, *The Idiot*, *The Possessed*, and *The Brothers Karamazov*. The novelist was one of the most profound Christian thinkers of the modern era and his *oeuvre* is prodigious. Our modest purpose here is to isolate a few of the central Christian themes in Dostoevsky's novels and to intimate why he is a prophetic voice, more urgently relevant than ever, in our own dark times.

Dostoevsky was one of the least abstract and least theoretical thinkers of the modern era. He was not one of the great system-builders, the architect of an imposing, methodically constructed and coherent structure of ideas such as we find in the work of people like Hegel, Marx, Darwin, and Freud. To be sure, there are recurrent themes and motifs, but there are also paradoxes, lacunae, digressions, obsessions, and puzzles, not to mention deep-seated and contradictory prejudices that sometimes disfigure his writing.[4] Dostoevsky's thinking proceeds not by way of rational argumentation but by a series of unpredictable detonations, illuminations, disturbances, incandescent eruptions. Intellectually speaking, his kindred spirits in the nineteenth century were Kierkegaard and Nietszche, and a little later, the Russian philosopher Nikolai Berdayev, thinkers sometimes herded together under the problematic term "existentialism." Dostoevsky's thinking is incarnated, made flesh and blood, in his characters and dramatized in his extraordinary narratives. To wrench Dostoevsky's ideas out of this fictional world—a world that often seems more immediate than what we take to be the "real world"—is to do them a terrible violence. But a short, abstracted introduction such as is being essayed here might provoke some readers to venture into this astonishing fictional world with its gallery of unforgettable characters—Raskolnikov and Sonya, Stavrogin, Kirillov, the Verkhovenskys, Prince Myshkin, Rogozhin and Nastasya Filippovna, the Karamazovs, Father Zosima, the Grand Inquisitor, and the Man from Underground—there to discover for themselves an understanding of the Christian vision that makes the work of most commentators, both defenders of the faith and its critics alike, look pallid by comparison.

At the heart of Dostoevsky's religious thought is the figure of

Christ Himself. Even the most casual student of the history of Christianity knows that its founder is a figure amenable to an astonishing diversity of "readings." Leave aside for the moment the theologians and philosophers—amongst whom there is no shortage of disagreement! A simple exercise: compare the representation of Christ in Holman Hunt's painting *The Light of the World*, the writings of St Thérèse of Lisieux or Simone Weil, Kazantzakis' novel *The Last Temptation*, Pasolini's film *The Gospel According to St Matthew*, the stage production *Jesus Christ Superstar*. Everything from "Jesus meek and mild" to a fiery and angry revolutionary. The extraordinary thing is that each answers to some aspect of Christ, understood not only as an historical figure but in his mythic, mystical, and cosmic dimensions. Dostoevsky never hazarded a fictional portrait of Christ Himself, nor did he engage in theological speculations. Rather, what he offers us is a series of Christ-like figures, or more precisely, characters in whom we discern Christ-like qualities. Most notable amongst these are Prince Myshkin, the enigmatic protagonist of *The Idiot*, a "fool in Christ," the *yurodivy* whose spiritual insight "operates instinctively, below any level of conscious awareness or doctrinal commitment."[5] The novelist remarked that he wanted to create a character that was "entirely positive . . . with an absolutely beautiful nature," a "true Christian." Pondering the difficulties of the task, Dostoevsky wrote:

> The novel's central idea is to portray the absolutely good person. There is nothing more difficult than this in the whole world, especially in our time. All authors—not only ours, but also all the European ones—who have attempted a portrayal of an absolutely good person, have always given up. . . . In the whole world there is only one absolutely good person: Christ, and consequently the very existence of this one infinitely good being is in itself an ineffable miracle. The entire Gospel according to St John came into being over this thought. . . .[6]

Myshkin is gentle, pure, sincere, innocent, completely free of guile and malice, full of pity and love, and taken by some of his contemporaries to be an idiot. He's also an epileptic (as was Dostoevsky), is devoted to the prostitute Nastasya Filippovna, in love with the passionate Aglaya Ivanovna, and given to outbursts about the evils of the West. Above all else, Myshkin, through his intuitive mystical insight and his deep and tender regard for his fellows, is the champion of "the insulted and the injured," sharing their suffering. He recalls the Jesus who consorts with thieves, lepers, prostitutes, and outcasts, the teacher of the Beatitudes. Some of these qualities (but by no means unalloyed) are also to be found in other characters who were close to Dostoevsky's heart—Sonya, Aloysha, Father Zosima, Marya Timofeevna. We find their polar opposites in characters who embody human pride, hypocrisy, egoism, and carnality: Raskolnikov, Svidrigaylov, Kirillov, the younger Verkhovensky, Stavrogin.

One of the most startling of Myshkin's characteristics is a *passivity* organically linked with his *suffering* and *humility*. This furnishes a key to Dostoevsky's understanding of Christ and His message. The ideal embodied in Myshkin "expresses itself in suffering rather than action, and subordinates action to feeling. The moral and psychological relation between [individuals] is all-important; the action which proceeds from it relatively indifferent. In the antinomy between feeling and action the West has constantly given the preference to the latter.... Yet it would not be hard to show that Dostoevsky more accurately represents the primitive Christian tradition of the gospels."[7] As E. H. Carr further notes, Christ's two great commandments and seven of the eight Beatitudes "enjoin not actions but states of feeling"—or perhaps we might better say "states of *being*." For Dostoevsky, the Christian way of love is one of *radical interiority*. Hence his implacable resistance to all forms of religious legalism and puritanical moralism, two maladies he identified with the Catholic and Protestant traditions of the West.

Dostoevsky's understanding of Christ is illuminated by his reaction to Holbein's painting *The Body of the Dead Christ in the Tomb*. While on their honeymoon in Europe, in 1867, Dostoevsky and his wife Anna visited the Basel Museum, where he was dumbstruck, nay traumatized, by this painting which in its grim and graphically naturalistic depiction of a damaged and decaying corpse challenged all notions of Christ's divinity. In *The Idiot* Myshkin echoes Dostoevsky's appalled state when he declares that "a man's faith might be ruined by looking at that picture!" As Joseph Frank, the doyen of Dostoevsky scholars, has written, "In Holbein the Younger, Dostoevsky sensed an impulse, so similar to his own, to confront Christian faith with everything that negated it, and yet to surmount this confrontation with a rekindled (even if humanly tragic) affirmation."[8] Or, as another commentator has put it, Dostoevsky was determined to "crash-test his Christian convictions." From his notebooks: "My Hosanna has burst forth from a huge furnace of doubt."[9] That searing confrontation with doubt and that hardearned affirmation is given perhaps its most powerful expression in the dialectic between Aloysha and Ivan in *The Brothers Karamazov*, culminating in one of the most memorable passages in Dostoevsky's entire corpus, the Grand Inquisitor's soliloquy. It is altogether characteristic of Dostoevsky's work that many readers find Ivan's atheistic and rationalistic arguments more compelling than those of Aloysha, which is to say that the novelist puts the case *against* his own position with tremendous honesty and force. Graham Greene did something of the same sort in the confrontation of the Lieutenant and the "whisky priest" in *The Power and the Glory*.

Dostoevsky returns explicitly to Holbein's painting in *The Idiot*. On encountering Holbein's painting, Ippolit, a tubercular young nihilist, cries out that "blind nature" (for which we can also read Fallen Man) has "senselessly seized, smashed and devoured, dully and without feeling, a great priceless Being, a Being worth all of nature and its laws, worth the whole Earth, which was created perhaps solely for the emergence of that Being."[10] Famously, and in characteristic fashion, Dostoevsky declared in one of his letters that, "If someone proved to me that Christ is outside the truth and that in reality the truth were outside of Christ, then I should prefer to remain with Christ rather than with the truth." Not a formulation to please rationalistic philosophers, but it tells us a great deal about Dostoevsky's soul. One of his friends in Siberia tells us that although Dostoevsky, generally, did not like priests and went to church infrequently, he was deeply pious, and that he reinvigorated his faith by looking at the stars, and that he always spoke about Christ "ecstatically."[11]

A century after Dostoevsky was writing *Crime and Punishment* and *The Idiot* another Orthodox thinker, Metropolitan Anthony (Archbishop Anthony Bloom, 1914–2003) rehearsed one of the novel's cardinal themes: "The loss of God is death, is desolation, hunger, separation. All the tragedy of man is in one word, 'godlessness.'"[12] For Dostoevsky the "loss of God" was *the* problem of the modern era. Three years after the publication of *The Brothers Karamazov* (1879) Nietzsche's *The Gay Science* appeared, announcing the "death of God." On the face of it this seemed to many to be a triumphant declaration, a cause for celebration, a decisive and epochal step forward in man's liberation from the fetters of religious superstition. But even for Nietzsche himself, the matter was a great deal more ambiguous, as is dramatized in the following passage:

> The madman jumped into their midst and pierced them with his eyes. "Whither is God?" he cried; "I will tell you. We have killed him—you and I. All of us are his murderers. But how did we do this? How could we drink up the sea? Who gave us the sponge to wipe away the entire horizon? What were we doing when we unchained this earth from its sun? Whither is it moving now? Whither are we moving? Away from all suns? Are we not plunging continually? Backward, sideward, forward, in all directions? Is there still any up or down? Are we not straying, as through an infinite nothing? Do we not feel the breath of empty space? Has it not become colder? Is not night continually closing in on us?"[13]

As Walter Kaufmann has written, Nietzsche "felt the agony, the suffering, and the misery of a godless world so intensely, at a time when others were yet blind to its tremendous consequence, that he was able to experience in advance, as it were, the fate of a coming generation."[14] Indeed, it may even be argued—though impossible to prove—that Nietzsche's proclamation of God's death was so unbearable that, in the end, it literally drove him mad. In any event, for Nietzsche "the death of God" was accompanied by a deep foreboding: "I foresee something terrible. Chaos everywhere. Nothing left which is of any value, nothing which commands: Thou shalt!"[15] We find the same premonition in Dostoevsky, for whom the crisis heralded by Nietzsche could only be overcome by a renewal of faith, by a deepening commitment to the universal message of Christ, and by a fidelity to the Orthodox Church and its mission. Nietzsche and Dostoevsky, along with the gloomy Dane, Søren Kierkegaard, fathomed the spiritual malaise of their time more deeply than any other nineteenth-century thinkers. Their diagnoses are marked by both striking convergences and divergences. Dostoevsky might easily have written, as Nietzsche did, "To have paced out the whole circumference of modern consciousness, to have explored every one of its recesses, this is my ambition, my torture and my bliss."[16] Incidentally, there is no evidence that Dostoevsky ever read anything by either Kierkegaard or Nietzsche, but we know that the latter was deeply affected by the Russian's work, declaring that Dostoevsky was the only psychologist from whom he had learned anything.

Pervasive in Dostoevsky's work is an inquiry into the nature of freedom, a subject he understands in a profoundly Christian way. In *Crime and Punishment*, Raskolnikov, a rebellious student and self-styled philosopher, intoxicated by European rationalism and individualism, elaborates a Nietzschean theory which posits that certain individuals are above moral and social laws, justified in expressing their self-willed freedom in whatever way they wish—in Raskolnikov's case the horrific murder of an elderly money-lending crone. Far from elevating Raskolnikov into an *Übermensch*, the murder hurls him into an inexorable spiral of ennui, guilt, and suicidal despair from which, ultimately, he is rescued by the pathetic Sonya, barely more than girl, thrown into prostitution by her family's predicament. In two pivotal scenes in the book Sonya reads to Raskolnikov the Gospel account of the resurrection of Lazarus. We understand that Raskolnikov's horrible ideology and his crime have dehumanized him, killed his soul, brought him to the state of the living dead. After Raskolnikov confesses his crime to Sonya she cries out, "What have you done, *what have you done to yourself?*" He asks Sonya what he must do: "Go at once, this very minute, stand at the cross-roads, bow down, first kiss the earth which you have defiled and then bow down to the whole world and say to all men aloud, 'I am a murderer!'" Thus begins Raskolnikov's repentance, his slow spiritual awakening and his painful journey back into the human fold. *Humility*, rooted in an awareness of our imperfect or "fallen" nature, an acceptance of *suffering* and its regenerative and transformative power, and a compassionate and sacrificial *love* for all of God's creation, especially our fellow humans, the least and most apparently worthless of whom are made in God's image, and whose lives are thereby sacrosanct—*these* are the ground of the only freedom worth the name. That freedom finds its highest and most sacred expression in compassion which, Dostoevsky wrote, "is the most important and possibly the only law for the whole of human life."[17] He works over the same problematic of the "will to power" and untrammeled "freedom" through the character of Kirillov in *The Possessed*, this time in a trajectory that ends not in redemption but in suicide, the logical endpoint of atheistic self-deification.

Another strand in Dostoevsky's thinking about freedom is that it must *necessarily* entail the existence of evil; if humans are truly free, as Dostoevsky believes, they must be free to sin, to do evil. But in *choosing* to do evil they betray the human vocation and condemn themselves to a spiritual imprisonment far worse than the kind of physical captivity and humiliation that Dostoevsky himself endured in Siberia. Evil, it might be said, is the price of freedom, a freedom that is the very hallmark of the human condition.

For Dostoevsky, the post-Enlightenment landscape in the West was a spiritual wasteland, over-run by profane ideologies and philosophies in various guises—the bland sentimentalities of the secular humanists, the complacencies of liberal progressivism, the dark romances of the Utopian revolutionaries, or the Promethean dream of the *Übermensch*, all anatomized with what George Steiner called "a gift of foresight bordering on the daemonic"[18] in *The Possessed*, all treacherous betrayals of our true nature as the sons and daughters of God. With chilling prescience Dostoevsky foreshadowed many of the pathologies of the twentieth century: the ennui and sterility of life in the industrial-capitalist-urban antheap, the mindless worship of false gods (progress, science, nation, power, money, hedonism), moral anarchy, the barbarities of totalitarianism, the "reign of quantity," the diabolical hubris of a scientism answerable to nothing. One of the most famous of Dostoevsky's lines comes in the words of Ivan Karamazov, "If God does not exist, everything is permitted"; it might well stand as the epitaph for the twentieth century.[19]

One of the most acute and sympathetic of all commentators on Dostoevsky is Nikolai Berdayev (1874–1978), theologian, philosopher, "Christian existentialist," and one of the heirs of Dostoevsky's religious vision. Let's give him the last word:

A careful reading of Dostoevsky is an event in life from which the soul receives a baptism of fire. The man who has lived for a time in Dostoevsky's world has seen as it were "unpublished forms" of being, for he is above all a great revolutionary of the spirit opposing himself to every kind of stagnation and hardening.[20]

Rudolf Otto

1869–1937

The Idea of the Holy and Religious Universalism

*"Holiness"—"the holy"—is a category of inter-
pretation and valuation peculiar to the sphere of religion.*[1]

n 1958 the appearance of a new edition of Rudolf Otto's *The Idea of the Holy* prompted *The London Quarterly Review* to commend the work as "an acknowledged classic." Mark Twain observed that a "classic" is a book that everyone praises and no one reads, which now seems to be the fate of *The Idea of the Holy* (1917). Otto's later writings on Eastern traditions and his efforts to fashion a new religious inclusivism are today also largely forgotten. A pity. After a brief overview and a few remarks about *The Idea of the Holy*, we will turn to Otto's encounters with Eastern religious traditions, and to his reconciliation of Christian theology and religious universalism.[2]

Otto was born in 1869 in Northern Germany, into a strict Lutheran family, the twelfth of thirteen children.[3] He describes the family milieu as "strictly burgherly and small town" and his school education as "not so pleasant and delightful as it otherwise usually is," due perhaps to his lack of friends and his "indifference" to the activities of his schoolmates. At quite a young age he determined to become a pastor and took a keen interest "in everything ecclesiastical and theological that managed to appear within my narrow horizons."[4] Otto studied theology, languages, music, and art at the universities of Erlangen and Göttingen. The young scholar was disenchanted with the "ossified intellectualism" of the prevailing rationalistic theology and was strongly attracted to Martin Luther's insistence that the knowledge of God had little to do with the rational faculties. Nearly half a century later Karl Barth recalled the uncongenial climate of German academic theology at that time:

> Everything that even from afar smelt of mysticism and morals, of pietism and romanticism or even idealism, how suspect it was and how strictly prohibited or confined in the straitjacket of restrictions.[5]

After two years in a theological seminary Otto traveled to the Middle East. In Cairo he was deeply moved by the Coptic liturgy, by some Jewish rites in Jerusalem, and by a Dervish ceremony that he described as "unspeakable." After these formative experiences he returned to Germany through the great monastic center at Mt Athos, where he spent ten days. This trip provided the catalyst for his first great intellectual enterprise, the construction of "a methodology of religious feeling."

Otto's professional life, apart from brief stints in the Lutheran ministry and as a Prussian Parliamentarian, was as a systematic theologian within the Academy. Throughout his adult life he engaged in a range of extra-academic activities including the movement for liturgical and ecclesiastical reform, the creation of ministries for women, electoral change, and efforts to establish an international Religious League. Ill-health forced his early retirement in 1929. He died of pneumonia in 1937, shortly after suffering an almost fatal sixty-foot fall from a tower he had climbed in Staufenberg. His last years were marred by severe illness, morphine addiction, depression, and perhaps more severe psychiatric disturbances; it is possible that Otto's "fall" was a suicide attempt.[6] The inscription on Otto's tomb in Marburg is *Heilig, Heilig, Heilig, ist der Herr Zaboath*, the *sanctus* that had taken on a particular resonance in his life and work.

Das Heilige appeared in 1917, in Europe a year of war, revolution, widespread dislocation, a mood of confusion, anxiety, and nihilism. It was to become one of the century's most influential books on the nature of religious experience, in some ways a descendant of William James's *The Varieties of Religious Experience* (1902). Soon translated into all the major European languages, it was immensely popular in the decade after its publication, perhaps because it answered to something in the mood of the times. *The Idea of the Holy* attempted to establish a category under which religious experience could be understood in its own right, free of any theoretical schema imported from outside. It was also an attempt to valorize the non-rational (as distinct from irrational) elements of religion. Otto's work was attuned to the spirit of Pascal's maxim,

> . . . if one subjects everything to reason our religion will lose its mystery and its supernatural character. If one offends the principles of reason our religion will be absurd and ridiculous. . . . These are two equally dangerous extremes, to shut reason out and to let nothing else in.[7]

In 1913 Otto's friend, the Swedish theologian Nathan Söderblom, had written, "Holiness is the great word in religion; it is even more essential than the notion of God."[8] Otto's purpose was to recuperate the full meaning of the word "holy" and to take hold of the religious experience to which it points. Otto believed the term had been contaminated by moral associations that were quite secondary to its fundamental meaning, and turned to an old Latin word, *numen*, to signal the realm of the most profound religious experience. The holy, he wrote, "is a category peculiar to religion ... [it] is perfectly *sui generis* and irreducible to any other; and therefore, like every absolutely primary and elementary datum, while it admits of being discussed, it cannot be defined,"[9] only evoked on the basis of experience. To experience the numinous is to encounter the *mysterium tremendum*, marked by an overpowering sense of otherness, of awefulness, majesty, and energy, but the *numen* is also *fascinans*—beautiful, alluring, captivating. This real presence, neither a phantom nor a projection of the sub-conscious but, in Christian terms, the "living God," calls up "creaturely feeling" and appears "in a form ennobled beyond measure where the soul held speechless, trembles inwardly to the furthest fibre of its being."[10] In an Appendix, Otto reproduces the thrilling passage from the *Bhagavad Gita* where Arjuna "smitten with amazement" beholds the manifold forms of Krishna, more dazzling than "the light of a thousand suns."

Part of the book's appeal was Otto's understanding of religion primarily in experiential rather than creedal terms. At a time when "religion" was often thought to hinge on belief and moral observance, Otto turned attention to the religious experience, not to offer any reductionistic "scientific" explanation but to affirm its mystery and power, and to insist on its centrality in religion. Comparative religionists were later to take up Otto's interest in the holy (now more often than not termed "the sacred") as one of the structuring principles of their inquiries.

In 1911 Otto traveled extensively in North Africa, the Middle East, and India: his experiences were to be decisive in the gestation of *The Idea of the Holy*. In a letter he described the effect of hearing the Trisagion of Isaiah in the synagogue in Moroccan Mogador (now Essaouira):

It is Sabbath, and already in the dark and inconceivably grimy passage of the house we hear that sing-song of prayers and reading of scripture, that nasal half-singing half-speaking which Church and Mosque have taken over from the Synagogue. The sound is pleasant, one can soon distinguish modulations and cadences that follow one another at regular intervals, like leitmotif. The ear tries to grasp individual words but it is scarcely possible... when suddenly out of the babel of voices, causing a thrill of fear, there it begins, unified, clear and unmistakable.... I have heard the *Sanctus Sanctus Sanctus* of the cardinals in St Peters, the *Swiat Swiat Swiat* in the Cathedral of the Kremlin and the Holy Holy Holy of the Patriarch in Jerusalem. In whatever language they resound, these most exalted words that have ever come from human lips always grip one in the depths of the soul, with a mighty shudder exciting and calling into play the mystery of the other world latent therein.[11]

As Ernst Benz observed, "It is particularly noteworthy that Otto came to know the experience [of the holy] not primarily from reading sacred texts but on a journey as a spontaneous religious experience in a Jewish synagogue in Morocco."[12] The Asian leg of his travels also left an abiding impression on Otto. Soon after arriving in Karachi he was astonished when a newly-met Hindu youth launched into an eloquent discourse on the philosophy of Kant. Otto sailed up the Indus River to Lahore and thence traveled to Calcutta and Orissa, where he was lavishly entertained by a Maharajah in whom he found an attractive blend of European learning and Hindu piety. In India he had friendly encounters with Muslims, Sikhs, Hindus, and Parsees. From India Otto traveled to Burma, where he was much impressed by the vitality of Theravadin Buddhism. In Japan he visited universities, temples, and monasteries and may have been the first Westerner to address a large gathering of Zen monks. He went on to China, where he stayed for two months before returning to Europe through Siberia, accompanied by a collection of priceless religious artifacts for the Museum of the World's Religions which he had established in Marburg.

Despite poor health, Otto returned to India in 1927 and visited many religious sites throughout the sub-continent; his letters evince a keen and sympathetic interest in the beliefs and practices of the

Buddhists, Muslims, and Parsees, as well as the Hindus. A visit to Elephanta Island near Bombay (now Mumbai), like his earlier experiences in the Middle East, left the most profound impression on him:

> One climbs halfway up the mountainside on magnificent stone steps until a wide gate opens on the right, in the volcanic rocks. This leads into one of the mightiest of early Indian rock temples. . . . The eye slowly accustoms itself to the semi-darkness, gradually distinguishes awesome representations—carved into the wall—of the religious epics of India, until it reaches the imposing central recess. Here an image rises up out of the rock which I can only compare with the great representations of Christ in early Byzantine churches. It is a three-headed form, carved only as far as the breast, in threefold human size. . . . Still and powerful the central head looks down, with both the others in profile. Over the image rests a perfect peace and majesty. . . . Nowhere else have I found the secret of the transcendent world, the other world more grandly and perfectly expressed than in these three heads. . . . To see this place were alone worth a journey to India, while from the spirit of religion which has lived here, one may experience more in a single hour of contemplation than from all the books.[13]

The last sentence is a telling sign of Otto's deepening conviction that "the spirit of religion" transcends all formal boundaries and lies in contemplative experience, beyond the reach of "all the books."

Otto was by now an accomplished Sanskritist, had translated several Vedic texts and published his most important contribution to the Western understanding of the Hindu tradition, *Mysticism East and West* (1926), in which he continued Schopenhauer's association of Vedantic metaphysics and Meister Eckhart's apophatic theology. Whilst not unaware of "manifold singularities," Otto found in the mystics of both East and West "an astonishing conformity in the deepest impulses of human spiritual experience," independent of "race, clime and age."[14] His work remains a pioneering work of remarkable acuity in the field of comparative mysticism.

In *The Idea of the Holy* Otto had already discussed the mystical dimension of religion in terms altogether consonant with the spiritual vocabularies of the East. Take this, for example:

And as soon as speculative thought has come to concern itself with this . . . type of consciousness. . . . We come upon the ideas, first, of the annihilation of the self, and then, as its complement, of the transcendent as the sole and entire reality. For one of the principal and most general features of mysticism is just this self-depreciation . . . the estimation of the self, the personal "I," as something not perfectly or essentially real, or even as a mere nullity, a self-depreciation which comes to demand its own fulfilment in practice in rejecting the delusion of selfhood, and so makes for the annihilation of the self.[15]

After this second trip to India, Otto wrote many scholarly works on the Vaisnavite tradition, translated several texts, including those of Ramanuja, the *Katha Upanishad*, and the *Bhagavad Gita*, with which he originally felt little sympathy but on which he was to write with great discernment.[16] Otto also wrote a comparative study, *India's Religion of Grace and Christianity* (1928). Much of his work served as a corrective to the Western preoccupation with Advaita Vedanta, often assimilated with the Hindu tradition as a whole. Of Otto's imposing Indological work, Joachim Wach, Otto's one-time student, had this to say:

All these studies not only bespeak an intimate acquaintance with the texts and the philological problems involved in their interpretation, not only a comprehensive knowledge of the theological and philosophical systems of India and of the outstanding Hindu thinkers and teachers, but also a deep understanding of Indian devotion.[17]

Given Otto's deep-seated interest in lived religious experience and his perception of the similarities between the theistic piety of the Abrahamic traditions and Hindu *bhakti*, it comes as no surprise that Wach should identify his understanding of devotion as one of the hallmarks of Otto's studies.

Amongst Otto's most interesting and penetrating essays was one on Gandhi whom Otto recognized as a distinctly Indian type.

True, Gandhi impresses us through his profound humanity, and we admire "the human" in him. But he is an Indian, and it is as a great Indian that he is a great person. . . . We misunderstand Gandhi when we attempt to understand the strong powers and virtues of this man simply in terms of a generalized humanity . . . "the great nationalist," "the friend of the people," "a clever politician," "a born leader." He is all these things, but he is so as an Indian sadhu [renunciate]. He is these things as a result of his situation, but if the situation were different, his character as a sadhu would remain the same and would find other ways to express itself.[18]

He also discerned in the Mahatma the beneficent influence of the various religions to which he had been exposed and to whose ethical teachings he was peculiarly receptive—Jainism, Islam, and Christianity, as well as his own Vaisnavite tradition.[19]

Although Otto was most strongly attracted to Hinduism, especially its medieval expressions, he also wrote sympathetically about Buddhism of both the Theravada and Mahayana traditions. His percipient essay (1924) on Zen Buddhism came at a time when it was virtually unknown in the West and followed his many suggestive references to Buddhism in *The Idea of the Holy*. Philip Almond tells us that Otto was the first German scholar of religion to visit Zen monasteries in Japan, where he conversed with Zen masters, practised *zazen*, addressed Zen monks on the affinities of Christianity and Buddhism, and lectured at the Asiatic Society of Japan on parallels between the religions of East and West.[20] At a time when any amount of nonsense was being written in the West about Buddhism, Otto's insights were penetrating indeed, and are still illuminating today. Unlike many Orientalists, Otto did not find Buddhism either "nihilistic" or "pessimistic" and in Zen discerned a radical mystical method, "almost torn away from all rational schemata," aimed at a direct encounter with the numinous, the "wholly other." In 1925 Otto wrote the preface to the first book on Zen in German and later an important essay, "Numinous Experience in Zen." He wrote very little on Islam, but even here one sees a remarkably plastic religious sensibility at work, one which allowed play to spontaneous aesthetic illuminations—not often to be found amongst academic theologians! How much of the spiritual economy of Islam Otto is able to evoke in a few deft strokes in his modest notes on "The empty in Islamic architecture" (1932):

Mosques are "empty." This is often confused with austerity and attributed to the alleged rationalism of Islam and its cultus. To be sure, there are mosques that are very austere, but there are others in which the empty speaks so impressively that it puts a lump in one's throat and takes one's breath away.... This high art works with space and through spaces that it orders, divides, and combines. At the same time it works with light, or rather, with half-light, which it wonderfully guides, gradates, mixes, augments, and interrupts. The use of both space and light makes the empty and the quiet meaningful and expressive. It does so without a word and more powerfully than cathedrals filled with images, figures, and ritual implements that diffuse, refract, and establish meaning through the all-too-significant and the all-too-conceptual.[21]

He describes Islamic calligraphy as "music with lines" that "draws the words of the *Quran* back into the mystery from which they flowed."

Otto often derived his most acute insights from direct existential encounters rather than from his researches in the library. Would that we could say the same of many of today's scholars of religion for whom the phenomena under investigation are like so many specimens on the laboratory bench, quite lifeless! As the Rumanian philosopher E.M. Cioran remarked, "One does not imagine a specialist in the history of religions at prayer. Or if indeed he does pray ... then he ruins his Treatises, in which no true god figures...."[22] Otto's intellect was as sharp as you like, his scholarship prodigious, and his capacity for argumentation formidable indeed; but perhaps more important than all this was a kind of intuitive receptivity shared by some of the century's most arresting Western commentators on Eastern religious traditions.

In the last two decades of his life Otto devoted himself to the creation of a *Religiöser Menschheitbund* (Interreligious League) that would bring together representatives of all the world's religions to work towards international peace, social justice, and moral progress. In the sorry aftermath of the Great War, Otto pleaded eloquently and passionately for the RMB:

I hope that the misery which all nations suffer today will finally teach them what religion and ethics should have taught them a long time ago: that they do not walk alone. People of every land and nation must constantly bear in mind that they face great collective tasks, and that to accomplish these tasks they need brotherly collaboration and cooperation. By themselves, political associations cannot do what is needed. . . . Will [the League of Nations] become anything more than a "limited liability corporation" that actively pursues the special interests of whatever groups temporarily find themselves in power. . . . In and of themselves, institutions, laws, decrees, and negotiations are powerless. They require the continual support of an awakened collective conscience. . . .

Otto strikes a very contemporary note in pressing the urgency of "issues of public and international morality, social, and cultural issues that all nations share, unavoidable clashes between different nations and how to alleviate them, issues of class, gender, and race."[23] Under Otto's leadership the RMB, established in 1920, actually flourished for a time before being dissolved in 1933. Whilst it failed to realize his lofty ideals, who is foolish enough to say that his vision has no relevance today? In a world riven with all manner of strife, much of it inter-religious, and at the end of the most bloodstained century in recorded history, perhaps it is timely to listen once again to Otto's impassioned words, uttered in the aftermath of the Great War:

If one could win the "churches" of the great world religions and their leaders for the cause of the great, common tasks of humanity—ordering relations between nations, classes, races, and genders in accordance with basic human rights; peaceful collaboration instead of war and aggression; reason and orderliness instead of the interests of those who are temporarily in power; the deliberate shaping of destiny instead of blindly allowing nature and destiny to take their course—then there would be created, in universal conviction and united opinion, the spiritual soil from which would grow lasting forms of international law and powerful organizations of nations and classes.[24]

Many will no doubt dismiss Otto's vision as "sentimental," "utopian," and the like; that is the fate of visionaries! But an implacable fact remains: Otto's appeal for the development of "a global conscience," rooted in the recognition of "the binding force of right and justice as the supreme norms governing relations between individuals and communities," and addressing the great, collective moral tasks of the age, cannot be indefinitely ignored without imperiling the very future of the human family and, indeed, of our planetary home.

Over the last century we can discern in the study of religion four distinct approaches, sometimes overlapping: the rationalistic perspective which treats religion like any other cultural phenomenon and strives for some sort of quasi-scientific "objectivity" (actually chimerical, but that is a debate for another occasion); the theological outlook which views "religion" and "religions" through the lens of a particular religious viewpoint; the universalist approach which rests on the notion that behind myriad religious forms lies some sort of common core or essence; and the phenomenological method which sets aside all questions relating to "truth claims" and seeks to allow the "phenomena" to somehow speak for themselves. Needless to say there are all manner of variations and off-shoots within these broad general groupings. Rudolf Otto is one of the first of a small group of Christian theologians who have attempted to reconcile their own fervent religious commitments with a more inclusive and universalist approach in the study of religion. As Seyyed Hossein Nasr observed many years ago, as far as religiously committed scholars are concerned,

> The essential problem that the study of religion poses is how to preserve religious truth, traditional orthodoxy, the dogmatic theological structures of one's own tradition, and yet gain knowledge of other traditions and accept them as spiritually valid ways and roads to God.[25]

Otto squarely faced the fact that Christian exclusivism must give way to a much more open approach to other religions. As early as 1912 he had struck a prophetic note with these noble words:

> We in the West now realize that we have no monopoly of religious truth. We must in honesty change our attitude towards other faiths, for our watchword must be "Loyalty to truth." This changed attitude, however, does not weaken, but rather, instead, reinforces one's faith in God, for He is seen to be not a small or partial being

but the Great God who is working throughout all times and places and faiths.[26]

Here Otto anticipates the work of later figures like Klaus Klostermaier, Henri Le Saux, Bede Griffiths, William Johnston, and Diana Eck, in each of whom we find a steadfast commitment to the Christian tradition hand-in-hand with the deepest respect for, interest in, and openness to, the spiritual modalities of other traditions. But none of this should be confused with the kind of "universalism" that anticipates the creation of a new "super-religion." Otto himself had no interest whatsoever in any kind of syncretism or admixture of religious elements in some sort of ersatz "universal" religion:

> We most emphatically reject any form of cosmopolitanism in the area of religion.... We maintain our religion and cherish its claims, at the same time that we allow others to advocate their own religion.... We consider the propagation and spreading of our own religion to be one of our most sacred duties....[27]

Although Otto's work has been strangely neglected in the Anglophone world over the last fifty years there is no doubting his influence on both theologians and comparative religionists. For many years Paul Tillich alone amongst German theologians really carried Otto's banner in the English-speaking world, but the climate today, in which "theologians now inhabit a world of religious pluralism, uncertain truth claims, and interreligious dialogue," may well make Otto's ideas congenial once again.[28] There can be no doubting that the ideals for which Otto strived and the values he upheld, both within the Church and in the wider world, have lost none of their pertinence or urgency.

Evelyn Underhill

1875–1941

On Mysticism

*The mystic lives and looks; and speaks the
disconcerting language of first-hand experience, not
the neat dialectic of the schools.*[1]

ardinal Newman is attributed with the aphorism that "Mysticism begins in mist and ends in schism," to which later sceptics have added that it also has an "i" in the middle. Whatever the provenance of the saying, it flags an attitude widespread among Christians in the nineteenth-century Anglophone world. The animus to "mysticism" was particularly strong in many Protestant circles. For many, not least the theologians, the term seemed more or less synonymous with "mystification," conjuring a dangerous realm of fantastical mumbo-jumbo, psychic disturbance, and unseemly disregard for theological orthodoxies. Even today the term often causes some discomfort, sometimes for reasons quite different from those that might have alarmed the cardinal. In some quarters, "mysticism," like "spirituality," has become a more or less meaningless buzz-word, sometimes conflated with various ideas derived from occultism and self-styled "esoteric" movements, not to mention the fatuities of the "New Age." But here is not the place to chart the shifts in meaning, connotation and association—some positive, some pejorative—which the term "mysticism" has undergone in the last century. Our purpose, rather, is to focus on a pivotal but now largely neglected figure who helped to re-valorize mysticism-proper and its central place in Christian life, Evelyn Underhill. Her most widely-read book, published in 1911, was *Mysticism: A Study of the Nature and Development of Man's Spiritual Consciousness*, followed by the more accessible *Practical Mysticism* (1914). The subtitle of the latter was *A Little Book for Normal People*, signposting her intention to bring mysticism out of the hermetic domain of theologians and scholars and into the purview of ordinary folk. One way or another, most of her forty-odd books and several hundred articles addressed this subject, her most abiding concern.

Before exploring several aspects of Underhill's work on mysticism let us recall a few biographical facts.[2] She was born into a well-heeled, religiously-indifferent, middle-class family in Wolverhampton, was largely home-educated, married a barrister, and traveled frequently to Italy and France, drawn thither by a fascination with the Catholic heritage of Europe. In her youth and early adulthood she was agnostic but had "abrupt experiences of the peaceful, undifferentiated plane of reality—like the 'still desert' of the mystic—in which there was no multiplicity nor need of explanation."[3] For a short while she was a member of the Hermetic Society of the Golden Dawn, where esoteric types and "adepts," many Theosophists and Freemasons amongst them, ventilated arcane subjects. One might rub shoulders with the likes of W.B. Yeats, A.E. Waite, Aleister Crowley, Conan Doyle, Dion Fortune, and Maud Gonne. If you were lucky you might indulge in some astral travel. The principal benefit for Underhill was the exposure to Eastern traditions and doctrines. A.E. Waite, one of Golden Dawn's leading lights, also encouraged her growing attraction to Roman Catholicism. Underhill's spiritual journey reached a significant turning point in 1907 when she spent a few days in retreat with a friend at a Franciscan convent. She found the pervasive atmosphere of piety and devotion so overpowering that she fled, but on the next day had a spontaneous visionary experience which, she said, had no specifically Christian coloration but which convinced her that Catholic teaching was true and that she would find her "ultimate home" in the Roman Church.[4] On the brink of marriage, in 1907, she determined to convert to Rome, but met with "a storm of grief, rage and misery" from her fiancé; his hostility and her own intellectual scruples about some Catholic teachings kept her in the Anglo-Catholic ranks of the Church of England until, late in life, she entered the Greek Orthodox Church. In middle-age she was much influenced by Baron Friedrich von Hügel (1852–1925), an Austrian-born Catholic philosopher who moved Underhill to a much more Christocentric understanding of the tradition as well as enriching her understanding of the various streams of Christian mysticism. Underhill formally placed herself under his spiritual directorship in the early 1920s and wrote that it was to him, "under God," that she owed her "whole spiritual life."[5] Her interest in the spiritual life generally and mysticism particularly became less exclusively scholarly and more experiential and pragmatic, a shift prompted by a decisive commitment to Christianity. In the 1920s she became an Anglican spiritual director and retreat leader. She was fond of cats. My collaborator Brian will be pleased to find that she was also an accomplished bookbinder. As well as her extensive writings on religion and spirituality she also produced several novels and volumes of poetry, and gave many public lectures and radio talks. In the last few years of her life she became an active pacifist and published *The Church and War* (1940).

Among her many interesting projects and collaborations was her partnership with Rabindranath Tagore in producing an anthology of the mystical poetry of Kabir. Another was her biography of Jacopone da Todi, a thirteenth-century Franciscan poet and mystic whose criticism of Pope Boniface VIII saw him imprisoned and excommunicated. Other lasting interests included Plotinus and neo-Platonism, the art and architecture of the Middle Ages, the work of William Blake, the arts and crafts movement, and medieval mystical literature, particularly *The Cloud of Unknowing* and Ruysbroeck, whom she compared to Hindu mystics, the Christian Neoplatonists, and Meister Eckhart, and in whose writings she found "the high water mark of mystical literature." The Flemish mystic she wrote,

> seems to exhibit within the circle of a single personality, and carry up to a higher term than ever before, all the best attainment of the Middle Ages in the realm of Eternal life. The central doctrine of the Divine Fatherhood, and of the soul's power to become the son of God, it is this raised to the nth degree of intensity . . . and demonstrated with the exactitude of the mathematician, and the passion of a poet, which Ruysbroeck gives us. The old mystic sitting under his tree seems here [in *The Sparkling Stone*] to be gazing at and reporting to us the final secrets of that eternal world.[6]

In later life she focused more on the spiritual path itself, writing extensively on such subjects as contemplation, prayer, and liturgy.

Before the appearance of *Mysticism*, Underhill had already published a volume of poetry, several novels, and *The Miracles of Our Lady Saint Mary*. But the new book inaugurated her far-reaching study of mysticism, primarily in its European expressions but not excluding the East. It also brought her work to a much wider reading public. Like William James's *Varieties of Religious Experience* (1903) and Rudolf Otto's *The Idea of the Holy* (1902), *Mysticism* quickly became more or less obligatory reading for anyone with a serious interest in religion. A century later a contemporary scholar, looking back, accented Underhill's focus on the universality of mystical experience:

Although it may be evaluated as rather naive by today's more sophisticated nuancing of the question of a universal mystical experience, *Mysticism* would be a pioneering study of the question of the universality of religious experience. As a refrain summarizing her belief about the commonality of such phenomena, Underhill quotes Saint Martin's aphorism that "all mystics speak the same language and come from the same country." As reflective of her own stage of commitment, her classic would mirror a more theistic rather than a specifically Christian perspective in the study of mystical consciousness. One would have to wait for *The Mystic Way* or other later writings to observe the Christian turn in her personal commitment.[7]

Important later works included *Ruysbroeck* (1915), *The Essentials of Mysticism* (1920), and *The Mystics of the Church* (1925).

"Mysticism": well, what is it? Here is one of Underhill's definitions:

> Mysticism, according to its historical and psychological definitions, is the direct intuition or experience of God; and a mystic is a person who has, to a greater or less degree, such a direct experience—one whose religion and life are centered, not merely on an accepted belief or practice, but on that which the person regards as first-hand personal knowledge.[8]

This workaday formulation deserves some attention. Firstly: "the direct intuition or experience of God" raises the vexed question "who or what is 'God'"? to which Underhill might reply that only the mystic knows, and knows only through direct participation in the Divine Nature. One might say that only God within us knows God, or, in the words of the Apostle, "The things of God knoweth no man, but the Spirit of God."[9] As the literature of both Occident and Orient testifies, in the mystical experience the subject-object distinction disappears, so that it is really no longer a question of what the mystic "knows" *about* "God." Mysticism, says Underhill, "is the art of direct union with Reality."[10] In the passage above the phrase "which the person regards as first-hand personal knowledge," spotlights a problem that has dogged the discussion of mysticism through the centuries: how are we to know that the "mystical" experience is not simply a matter of subjective self-deception, a chimera arising out of subconscious neuroses and urges—"wish-fulfilment" and "consolation" as Freud would have it. The question troubled Underhill herself. In a letter she confessed to moments of doubt when she was overtaken by "a terrible, overwhelming suspicion that after all my 'spiritual experience' may only be subjective . . . . There is no real test."[11] Like most mystics she had her own "dark nights of the soul." However, it may be observed that the problem of "verifi-cation," if we might call it that, does not arise in the case of the ple-nary mystical experience: history is replete with examples where the experience in question has produced implacable and adamantine certitude about the suprasensible Reality—called by many names—which has been "experienced." The third feature of this passage to note is Underhill's reference to the "historical and psychological def-initions" of mysticism, alerting us to some of the limitations of Underhill's approach. Historical and psychological analyses raise the age-old problem—rampant in studies of religious phenom-ena—of trying to "explain" the greater in terms of the lesser. The movements of the Spirit altogether escape the grasp of a profane psychology, while historical inquiries do little more than contextu-alize various ideas and provide a kind of genealogy, possibly useful but unable to fathom the subject of mysticism. Ultimately the only adequate framework is provided by theology in its highest reaches or, if one wants a more universal perspective, by metaphysical doc-trines which subsume this or that theological viewpoint. Metaphys-ical doctrine is really the "objective" and impersonal dimension of *gnosis*—the knowledge of divine realities—to which the subjective illumination gives access. (The problematic nature of terms such as "subjective" and "objective," even "experience," might be surmised from the earlier remarks about the annihilation, in the full mystical experience, of the subject-object distinction.[12])

One may speak of various degrees of mystical apprehension, ranging from fugitive epiphanies and intimations up to those in which the egoic subject has altogether disappeared. One of the more common experiences is sometimes rather loosely called "nature mysticism," entailing an overwhelming sense of the Divine Presence in the world around us in the here and now, God immanent in time and space. Indeed, nearly everyone has experienced these kinds of momentary ruptures in our mundane consciousness. The beauty of the natural world is, after all, a reverberation of Divine Beauty. For Underhill the visible material world is a kind of shadow of the invisible world:

> For the most part, of course, the presence of the great spiritual universe surrounding us is no more noticed by us than the pressure of air on our bodies, or the action of light. Our field of attention is not wide enough for that; our spiritual senses are not sufficiently alert. Most people work so hard at developing their correspondence with the visible world, that their power of correspondence with the invisible is left in a rudimentary state.[13]

The "spiritual universe" really signifies Divine Immanence in which the world is, so to speak, suspended and which is immediately accessible if our "spiritual senses" are awakened.

It is often said that the mystical experience is "ineffable"; it is unutterable, cannot be expressed in words. Lao-Tze declared that "He who knows does not speak; he who speaks does not know"… but went on to speak at some length in the *Tao Te Ching!* This paradox—the attempt to express the inexpressible—reappears throughout history. Underhill concedes the problem, suggesting that the mystic who feels a compulsion to communicate the experience must do so through the use of symbol and image to create "some hint or parallel which will stimulate the dormant intuition of the reader."[14] She well understood that symbolism is the natural language of the mystic, for it is only by way of analogy that one can speak at all about suprasensible realities. All mystical language, we might say, is metaphorical.

Underhill's writings about mysticism are lively, well-informed, wide-ranging, intelligible, and a most useful support for many Christian wayfarers. But they are also marred by some of the prejudices of the period. To adduce a few of the tell-tale signs: a surrender to one of the most pernicious ideas of modern times, spiritual evolutionism (though her case seems to have been comparatively mild); the altogether confused notion that mystical experience can be understood and explained psychologically, this indicating the very common failure amongst modern commentators to distinguish between the spiritual and the psychic domains; the undue influence in her work of some sentimental "romantic" influences and of the ephemeral ideas of Henri Bergson's "vitalist" philosophy. As Michael Ramsey later noted, some of Underhill's writings on mysticism, particularly the earlier ones, are naïve and immature, "reflecting the weaknesses of the revival of mystical religion in the early years of this century," sometimes tinged with what Rowan Williams called the middle-class "cosiness" that has long beset the Anglican Church. Certainly there are more authoritative commentators on mysticism.

Perennialist writers such as Frithjof Schuon, Ananda Coomaraswamy, Martin Lings, and William Stoddart have provided us with accounts of mysticism in its various aspects (as experience, as doctrine, as path) that are both more comprehensive and more profound than anything we can find in Underhill's writings. They more adequately explain why "mysticism cannot not be," as it answers to what is "supernaturally natural" to humankind and thus lies at the heart of all religion.[15] These traditionalist writings do not exclude, but are not exhausted by, Christian understandings, which is to say they provide us with a more universalist viewpoint from which mysticism might be considered. Frithjof Schuon usefully defines the word "mystical" as "concerning universal realities considered subjectively: that is, in relation to the contemplative soul, insofar as they enter into contact with it."[16] Martin Lings clears away some of the confusions that have clouded many discussions of mystical doctrine (essentially metaphysics) when he states that it

> has the right to be inexorable because it is based on certainties and not on opinions. It has the obligation to be inexorable because mysticism is the sole repository of Truth, in the fullest sense, being above all concerned with the Absolute, the Infinite, and the Eternal; and "If the salt have lost its savor, wherewith shall it be salted?" Without mysticism, Reality would have no voice in the world. There would be no record of the true hierarchy, and no witness that it is continually being violated.[17]

For a short and lucid account of what mysticism is, and what it is not, readers might profitably turn to William Stoddart's essay, "Mysticism," in a splendid but little-known anthology of perennialist writings, *The Unanimous Tradition*.[18] Stoddart provides some correctives to Underhill's disproportionate reliance on historicist and psychologistic modes of understanding and interpretation. But whatever the limitations of her treatment, Underhill wrote in straightforward terms about the importance of the mystical experience and the imperative of contemplation in spiritual life, making these sometimes remote subjects accessible to ordinary folk. Underhill's achievement in *Mysticism* and in her subsequent books was *not* to give us an authoritative account of the subject, a task that could only be accomplished by a fully realized gnostic in the proper sense of the word, capable of articulating an adequate metaphysical doctrine—in the Christian tradition one may mention such figures as Pseudo-Dionysius, Meister Eckhart, and St Theresa of Avila as exemplars. It is hardly a criticism to point out that Underhill was not a figure of this kind. None of this means we should discard her work, in which there is much that is interesting, illuminating, and, indeed, beautiful. Nor should it blind us to Underhill's real achievement, which was to put mysticism back on the agenda, as it were. In the Preface to the twelfth edition of *Mysticism* (a book that has remained continuously in print for over a century) Underhill observed that

> Since this book first appeared, nineteen years ago, the study of mysticism—not only in England, but also in France, Germany, and Italy—has been almost completely transformed. From being regarded, whether critically or favorably, as a by-way of religion, it is now more and more generally accepted by theologians, philosophers and psychologists, as representing in its intensive form the essential religious experience of man.[19]

She was too modest to make the justifiable claim that her own book had played a seminal role in this transformation. It might be said, by way of a not altogether unambiguous tribute, that she popularized "mysticism." In the English-speaking world in the three decades following the publication of *Mysticism* she was one of the most widely-read authors on this subject. She played a vital role in what has been called "the mystical revival" in Protestant England in the first decades of the century, and introduced many readers, on both sides of the Atlantic, to the classics of medieval and Catholic spirituality, hitherto largely ignored by Protestants who also, in general, were quite ignorant of the mystical stream within Protestantism itself. Archbishop Ramsey again: "in the twenties and thirties there were few, if indeed any, in the Church of England who did more to help people to grasp the priority of prayer in the Christian life and the place of the contemplative element within it."[20] For these several beneficent and therapeutic influences she deserves our respect and gratitude. In the Preface to the twelfth edition of *Mysticism* Underhill suggested that all who wished "to make valid additions to our knowledge of the conditions under which the human spirit has communion with God" should approach the subject of mysticism with "truth-loving patience, with sympathy, and above all with humility."[21] It was in just such a spirit that she conducted her own work. Here she is writing about the soul sunk in the contemplative and prayerful love of God:

> Nothing in all nature is so lovely and so vigorous, so perfectly at home in its environment, as a fish in the sea. Its surroundings give to it a beauty, quality, and power which is not its own. We take it out, and at once a poor, limp, dull thing, fit for nothing, is gasping away its life. So the soul sunk in God, living the life of prayer, is supported, filled, transformed in beauty, by a vitality and a power which are not its own.[22]

A. P. Elkin

1891–1979

Anthropologist of High Degree

In Aboriginal thought man is twofold. He is visible body, but he is also spirit. The latter is invisible except to those with special sight.[1]

dolphus Peter Elkin was twenty-seven years old and a curate in a country parish in the Anglican Diocese of Newcastle when he visited the remote northwest of NSW, "back of Bourke."[2] There he was fascinated by archaic indigenous artefacts, occupation sites, and burial grounds. He was soon reading widely about all aspects of Aboriginal culture. At that time there were no university programs in archaeology, but Elkin was able to enrol in a Masters degree with Aboriginal religion as the subject of his thesis. Thus began an inquiry that was to last for the rest of his life. In 1919 he was appointed vice-warden of St John's Theological College in Armidale, at that time under the direction of the charismatic E.H. Burgmann. (Forty years later my father left the Methodist ministry in Melbourne to join the Anglican Diocese of Canberra and Goulburn in 1959, attracted thereto by Bishop Burgmann.) By 1925 Elkin had resigned from his post at St. John's and fully immersed himself in Aboriginal researches in the Kimberley and South Australia, and more formal study in London, Europe, and North America. After a spell as Warden of St John's College, now relocated to Morpeth, a suburb of Maitland (his birthplace), Elkin was appointed as Professor of Anthropology at Sydney University. He was soon occupying a variety of high-powered official positions, many of them concerned with government policy. Amongst these were the presidency of the Association for the Protection of Native Races and the vice-presidency of the NSW Aborigines Protection Board. He became a tireless activist in championing Aboriginal interests and rights as he understood them. He was altogether indefatigable in exposing and remedying injustices that issued from racist misconceptions, from governmental and judicial indifference and incompetence, and from the pervasive ignorance about Aboriginal culture. One of the best-known of such involvements was Elkin's successful campaign in 1933 to overturn the death sentence passed on Tuckiar, an Aboriginal man accused of killing a white man in the Northern Territory.[3] In his introduction to Bill Harney's book, *Taboo* (1949), after recalling several blood-stained encounters, Elkin remarks,

> Incidents such as these have occurred all too frequently in our "peaceful" conquest of the aborigines and their country. There has

been misunderstanding on both sides, much callousness, selfish-
ness and indifference on our part, and more than a fair share of
hardship, suffering and death on the part of the aborigines.[4]

Elkin was a prolific writer and contributed numerous articles to
Oceania, of which he was also the editor for more than forty years.
His most important works were *The Australian Aborigines: How to
Understand Them* (1938)[5] and *Aboriginal Men of High Degree* (1946).
He wrote eight books in all, one a book of personal reminiscences,
Morpeth and I (1937), another a church history, *The Diocese of New-
castle* (1955). His biographer has summed up his work in the field of
Aboriginal scholarship and public policy-making this way:

> As an anthropologist, he was a meticulous observer and recorder,
> with a particular interest in ritual and kinship; in terms of theory,
> he was a functionalist, a diffusionist, a Darwinist. In his religious
> beliefs, he was a humanist—in the tradition of his heroes Freder-
> ick Maurice and Charles Kingsley. As a lobbyist for the rights of
> Aborigines, he believed in the politics of compromise, courtesy
> and restraint; he proved tenacious in method and optimistic in
> outlook. Elkin regarded protection as the basis for growth and
> considered that Aborigines would inevitably be assimilated by
> White Australia (although he did not envisage them losing their
> identity in the process). He was a pragmatist, a plain speaker, a
> conservative who believed there was no point wasting energy on
> battles that could not be won.[6]

What manner of man was Elkin? He was tall, thin, "bird-like," ener-
getic, a work-obsessive, authoritarian, opinionated, intractable and
prickly, fiercely committed to his own vision of the Aboriginal
future. He could be an implacable and sometimes unpleasant oppo-
nent, as he showed in his uncharitable campaign against C. P.
Mountford, the leader of the 1948 Arnhem Land Expedition.[7] He
was a chap you didn't want as an enemy. Elkin ruled his own department at Sydney University with an iron fist and with "Machiavellian
efficiency." He was dedicated to public service, sharing J. S. Mill's
belief that "The most important point of excellence which any form
of government can possess is to promote the virtue and intelligence
of the people themselves. The first question in respect to any political institutions is how they tend to foster in the members of the

community the various desirable qualities . . . moral, intellectual and active" (*Considerations on Representative Government*). One of Elkin's favorite maxims was Cicero's injunction commending "inward satisfaction without outward show." He had what one commentator has called "an exacting commitment to the triad of religious faith, civic obligation and scientific endeavour."[8] In his private life he was a man with the now unfashionable attributes of rigid self-discipline and strict moral probity. He enjoyed playing tennis. In 1922 he married an Irish nurse whom he met during the influenza epidemic. Unfortunately, Elkin's biographer tells us little about her. In any event, Sally survived fifty-seven years of what seems to have been a happy marriage. They named the first of their two sons after the Christian socialist, Charles Kingsley, a durable influence on Elkin's outlook and social philosophy. Throughout his life Elkin suffered from many illnesses and ailments, some of them probably of nervous and stress-related origin. Like his prose and his speaking style, Elkin's personality seems to have been rather colorless. He didn't have a big joke-book and I don't expect he was that much fun at a party.

Why should anyone outside the field of anthropology be interested in Elkin's work? Well, before answering that question directly, let me start with a personal reminiscence. In 1968 I was a callow young student at the ANU, now in the last year of an Honors degree in history. My Honors thesis was entitled *The Science of Man* with the rather cumbersome subtitle "Scientific Opinion on the Australian Aborigines in the late 19th Century: The Impact of Evolutionary Theory and Racial Myth." It was only when I was well into my researches that I understood how inextricably intertwined and inseparable were "evolutionary theory" and "racial myth," a salutary and never-forgotten lesson about the vaunted "objectivity" of purportedly "scientific"" theories of one kind and another. My research focused on the evolutionary and anthropological theories of such heavies as Darwin himself, E.B. Tylor, Lewis Henry Morgan, J.G. Frazer, and Herbert Spencer, and on the impact of their work on Australian anthropologists like Bonwick, Fison and Howitt, R.H. Mathews, Spencer and Gillen, and T.G. Strehlow. Ultimately I was interested in the ways in which these ideas had affected popular perceptions and attitudes to Australia's indigenous people and their culture. My studies were guided by my supervisor, David Johanson, whose expertise included the history of the White Australia policy, and John Mulvaney in the ANU Research School, Australia's leading authority on the history of Australian anthropology. A decade later my primary intellectual concern had shifted to the field of comparative religion. While studying at Sydney University I rekindled my interested in the mythico-religious heritage of the Aborigines.

In both my ANU years and more forcibly at Sydney University I was struck by several conspicuous features of much of the literature in the broad field of Aboriginal studies, particularly in respect to spiritual life: the tyrannical grip of Darwinian evolutionary theory not only in its palaeontological-biological guise but in its bastard-child, the even more sinister "Social Darwinism"; the relentlessly reductionistic bent of much anthropological theorizing, fueled by the materialistic and progressivist assumptions of its exponents; the failure to approach indigenous doctrines, myths, and rituals in anything other than heavily Eurocentric terms; the malignant legacy in the national psyche of this complex of pseudo-scientific ideas. It was my good fortune to discover some powerful antidotes to these crippling circumscriptions in the work of a small handful of writers and scholars whose work was informed by a more acute understanding of these problems and a more open and sympathetic receptivity to what I came to think of as "the lessons of the nomads." The most helpful of these figures were Elkin himself, John Mulvaney, and W. E. H. Stanner, at one-time Elkin's pupil. In 1965, Stanner, surveying the anthropological literature, wrote this:

> It is preposterous that something like a century of study, because of rationalism, positivism, and materialism, should have produced two options: that Aboriginal religion is either (to follow Durkheim) what someone called "the mirage of society" or (to follow Freud) the "neurosis of society."[9]

Somewhat later I was to come across the work of James Cowan, whom I regard as the most percipient of all non-Aboriginal commentators on the religious life of the continent's first inhabitants. A brief account of Cowan's work comes later in the present volume. I should also mention the fact that in the years following my Honors research, my understanding of primordial cultures had been radically revised by the writings of the perennialists, especially René Guénon, Ananda Coomaraswamy, and Frithjof Schuon, and those of the maestro of the comparative study of archaic traditions, Mircea Eliade. Eliade himself never visited Australia nor, as far as I know, ever met an Aboriginal person. But he was able to write *Australian Religions* (1971), a fragmentary book that nonetheless contains a wealth of insights nowhere to be found in the anthropological literature. In more recent times I again encountered many of the problems mentioned above, this time in an American context, when I came to write about the life of the Lakota visionary, Black Elk.

Let's turn specifically to Elkin. Three-quarters of a century have passed since Elkin produced the work which marked the zenith of his researches, *Aboriginal Men of High Degree.* The intervening years have seen all sorts of changes in our understanding of indigenous cultures and in the situation of Australian Aborigines. Many of these changes have doubtless been for the better. It is inevitable that much of Elkin's work is now outdated and vulnerable to quite severe criticism when examined from our contemporary vantage-point. Indeed, during his own lifetime Elkin was not without his critics. Some of these were petty-minded anthropologists in academia who made much of Elkin's lack of professional training— which, in fact, was actually a blessing insofar as Elkin did not conform to many of their conventions and assumptions. Elkin's own Christian commitments were often adduced as evidence of his "biased" treatment of Aboriginal subjects, as if atheistic materialists were better equipped to understand the mysteries of the Dreamtime! But others were unhappy, understandably, about some of Elkin's assimilationist ideas and his generally conciliatory approach to white-black relations. As his biographer observes in her *Australian Dictionary of Biography* entry,

> As Elkin grew older and Aboriginal activism increased, his attitudes were severely criticized. Many saw his assimilation policy as weakening Aboriginality. Many interpreted his work on the Aborigines Welfare Board as meddling interference. Others felt he

should have been more confrontationist, more opposed to authority, more aggressive in dealing with White racists when championing the Aborigines of the Northern Territory and the Kimberleys.
This was not his way. He believed in adaptation—that all human
beings must adjust to their circumstances—White must adapt to
Black, and Black to White.

It is also true that Elkin's work was marred by Darwinian assumptions and by attitudes that we would now disavow as paternalistic,
assimilationist, and ameliorist. But criticizing the "sins of the
fathers" whilst ignoring the historical context in which these trans-
gressions took place, is not only an easy business but also an odious
one when fueled by a self-righteous complacency assuming that
now, of course, we enlightened ones know better. The prejudices of
one period are all too often dismantled only to be replaced by
newly-fashionable but unrecognized biases. So, my purpose here is
not to dwell on the indubitable limitations of Elkin's work but to
honor what was best in it.

Perhaps Elkin's principal contribution to the study of Aboriginal
religion was his heroic attempt to approach the phenomena (myths,
doctrines, rituals, customs, and so on) *in their own terms,* to treat
them as valid expressions of a mythopoeic and religious sensibility
rather than as either an ignorant and savage heathenism that must
give way to higher religious forms (i.e., Christianity) or as mere
epiphenomena of underlying forces understood either sociologi-
cally or psychologically, as in Durkheim's widely circulated dictum,
"The Aboriginal God is the dead chief," a formulation that anticipates the contemporary obsession in the so-called social sciences
with "power-relations" (Foucault lurking close by). Elkin rejected
both the evangelizing posture of many of his co-religionists and the
"scientific" pretensions of his professional colleagues to adopt what
comparative religionists would later term a "phenomenological"
method in which, insofar as possible, one "bracketed" or "put aside"
beliefs, values, and attitudes that were foreign to the people in question, an approach that foregrounded the *self-understanding* of the
religious practitioners in question. This was no easy task and no
doubt there was often a gap between aspiration and execution. The
fact remains that Elkin was remarkably open and sympathetic to the

ways in which indigenous people, especially the shamanic elders, understood their own beliefs and practices. He earned a deep respect from many of his informants. This was particularly important in his pioneering study of the most esoteric, occult, and inaccessible domain of Aboriginal tradition, the training and the practices of the *karadji*, in Western terms "medicine-men" or "clever men/women" or "shamans"; Elkin's own apposite term was "men of high degree." (The significant role of *women* of "high degree" remained a largely unknown country, but several of his students were to be trail-blazers on this front; one may mention figures such as Phyllis Kaberry, Camilla Wedgwood, Olive Pink, and Catherine Berndt.) Elkin's own Christian beliefs and commitments were unwavering, but they rarely intrude into his anthropological discourse.

The *karadji*, in Elkin's view, were "stewards of the mysteries," to be accorded the deepest respect. Here was an arcane realm of such things as "soul-flight," the initiatic "death-in-life" of the apprentice, of visionary experience, the gift of foretelling and telepathy, of other paranormal psychic powers quite beyond the reach of "empirical" and "data-based" research and consequently often dismissed by anthropologists as so much hocus-pocus that could only be explained in non-religious terms—for instance, as mere opportunistic paraphernalia created to camouflage *political* chicanery, part of a non-religious *agenda* and a stealthy *apparatus*. Elkin resisted the intransigent reductionism of his colleagues and committed the professional sin of taking these phenomena *seriously*! With acute insight Elkin compared aspects of Aboriginal shamanism with that of Hindu yogis and the adepts of Tibetan Buddhism.[10] Many of his intuitions about the *karadji* foreshadowed what later became the standard comparative work, Mircea Eliade's magisterial *Shamanism: Archaic Techniques of Ecstasy* (1951).

Of course there were many factors apart from the work of professional anthropologists fueling the slow transformation of European perceptions and attitudes; another was the work of popular writers about the bush and the outback, several of whom wrote about Aboriginal culture with sympathy and insight. One might mention figures such as Bill Harney, author of several books on tribal life, including *Life Among the Aborigines* (1957) and *Grief, Gaiety and Aborigines* (1961); Colin Simpson, author of *Adam in Ochre* (1951); and Douglas Lockwood, who wrote *I, the Aboriginal* (1962), the autobiography of Waipuldanya from the Roper River. Nor should we forget the influence of novelists as varied as Arthur Upfield, Katharine Susannah Prichard, Xavier Herbert, and Thomas Keneally. Bill Harney is a particularly interesting character: bushman, gold prospector, boundary rider, wrangler, trepang hunter, jailbird, cattle worker, husband to an Aboriginal woman, park ranger, peerless raconteur, a man with a deep, intelligent, and sympathetic interest in all aspects of Aboriginal life. He played a vital role as one of Elkin's most useful informants. The two became great friends and collaborated on *Songs of the Songmen* (1949), whilst Elkin wrote introductions to two of Harney's other books. Elkin told broadcaster John Thompson that if he knew as much as Harney did about Aboriginal culture he would spend the rest of his life at his desk writing. Unhappily, Harney's writings have fallen into neglect, partly because the contemporary sensitivity to racially-tinged language has occluded what is most insightful and valuable in his work.[11] (For better reason something of the same fate befell Jock McLaren's vivid account of his life on the Gulf of Carpentaria, *My Crowded Solitude*, first published in 1926 and regarded for some time as an Australian "classic.")

Not long after Elkin's death an American scholar in comparative religion, William Paden, wrote the following:

> Religions do not all inhabit the same world, but actually posit, structure, and dwell within a universe that is their own. They can be understood not just as so many attempts to explain some common, objectively available order of things "out there," but as traditions that create and occupy their own universe. Acknowledging these differences in place, these intrinsically different systems of experiencing and living in the world, is fundamental to the study of religion.[12]

Nowhere is this truer than in the study of primal cultures such as those of the Aborigines. This insight was not shared by many in Elkin's lifetime; it is very much to his credit that he honored this principle in his anthropological work. It should be added that

Paden's formulation should not be misconstrued to mean that religions are no more than "cultural productions," a fatal misapprehension to which even comparative religionists are not immune. Nor does it mean that diverse religious forms cannot reveal a supra-formal truth.

Elkin's contribution to the enrichment of our understanding of the Aboriginal tradition is more fully understood against the background of progressivist assumptions and attitudes that *still* plague European perceptions to this very day, even amongst those who are most keenly and painfully aware of the many injustices that have been heaped on our indigenous peoples. Whatever steps forward are evident in more open-minded attitudes and a more sympathetic understanding, many Australians are still lamentably ignorant about the continent's indigenous peoples, and racist prejudices and jaundiced stereotypes, sometimes more subtle than in days gone by, persist. Ideas and attitudes that were once almost universal amongst the whites are buried deep in the collective psyche and not simply swept away by good will or shallow political pieties. No, the problem is much more recalcitrant. Even amongst better-educated folk, free of at least the crude forms of racial prejudice, there remains one massive obstacle to a proper understanding of primal cultures, an impediment just as likely to face the historian, the anthropologist, and the sociologist as "the man or woman in the street": the deeply entrenched belief in "Progress" and the often unacknowledged or camouflaged notion that the prevailing way of life of the modern West (liberal democracy, the rule of law, capitalism, materialist science, industrial technology, the nuclear family, computers, mobile phones, Netflix) is, when all is said and done, an "advance" on the "backward" cultures of yesteryear. The idea of Progress is one of the most potent shibboleths of modernity, a kind of pseudo-myth. It comes attired in many alluring guises, often hand-in-hand with its malign accomplices, social and spiritual evolutionism, and finds applications in many fields. So pervasive is this idea in the modern climate, so much taken for granted, that it has become almost invisible, rather like the smog to which urban dwellers become inured. No doubt the unprecedented barbarisms of the last century and the atrocities and dislocations of the twenty-first have caused some disenchantment, but the tenacity of the idea is quite bizarre. "Progress" has a long and sordid pedigree in Western thought, and many brutalities and infamies have been justified in its name—the obliteration of the nomadic cultures is but one of them, the rape of nature another.

As a growing number of people are coming to realize, any liberation from the dire predicaments we presently face may only come by way of recourse to the ancient wisdom of which the Aborigines were such faithful custodians. Elkin would not have understood the matter in quite these terms, but it is fair to say that he is one of that small number who germinated this idea long before it became fashionable. Whatever else might be said about Elkin's work, this legacy is one for which we should be immensely grateful. Elkin's work was pivotal in bringing about a fundamental change in public perceptions whereby Aboriginal culture came to be understood not as the "dying remnants" of the Stone Age but "as an enduring and distinct aspect of Australian society."[13] Late in his life a friend wrote from Central Australia telling him of the revival of traditional "medicine-men" practices and ceremonies that gave him great joy. He responded to this news with the observation, "For I have seen a miracle. Aboriginal culture is not lost, merely changing."[14]

Dorothy Sayers

1893–1957

"A passionate intellect"

The dogma of the Incarnation is the most dramatic thing about Christianity, and indeed, the most dramatic thing that ever entered the mind of man; but if you tell people so, they stare at you in bewilderment.[1]

he Dorothy L. Sayers Society website lists no fewer than thirteen biographies of the English playwright, detective-story writer, poet, translator, social commentator, and Christian apologist. These days she is most often remembered as the author of fourteen books featuring the amateur sleuths Lord Peter Wimsey and Harriet Vane, enormously popular in their day but still selling well, as indeed are many of her other works. The Amazon listing of her books still available in various editions runs to some 75 pages. Nonetheless, it is fair to say that her star has somewhat faded, certainly so far as our literary cognoscenti are concerned: her sensibility and her preoccupations strike some as "old-fashioned," a bit musty, certainly not "cutting-edge." This is an unhappy state of affairs. A serious-minded consideration of her work reveals that whatever changing fashions might have done to obscure her work, her central concerns retain their pertinence. Sayers herself believed that imaginative literature could convey truths of a larger order than could more prosaic works in the other domains in which she expressed herself—social and political commentary, philosophy, theology. I have no quarrel with this position in principle but in Sayers' case I don't believe it applies. The brief discussion that follows foregrounds her work as a Christian apologist and social critic—not only one of the most lively and interesting of her time, but one of continuing relevance.

Given the contours of Sayers' life and thought it was perhaps appropriate, in an anticipatory sense, that she was born in the Headmaster's house, occupied by her father, at Christ Church School in Oxford. She was the only child of the Rev. Henry and Mrs Sayers, he of Anglo-Irish descent, she from a family of landed gentry. Dorothy won a scholarship to Somerville College, Oxford, graduating with first class honors in modern languages and medieval literature. She was later to be acclaimed for her translation of *The Divine Comedy*, which she herself believed (wrongly!) to be her most important work. The last of her works published in her own lifetime was a translation of *The Song of Roland*. She worked in publishing and copywriting (credited with the slogan "It pays to advertise"), then in various teaching posts in England and France before publishing her first Peter Wimsey story at the age of thirty, launching her career as a prolific novelist, essayist, playwright, journalist, and broadcaster. After a passionate but unconsummated and doomed relationship with a Jewish-Russian émigré poet she fell pregnant to another man (married, unbeknownst to her), and gave birth to an "illegitimate" son who was later legally adopted by Captain Oswald Fleming, a Scottish journalist whom she married in 1926. As Sayers' literary reputation grew she became friendly with the likes of C.S. Lewis (whose work she generally admired apart from some "shocking nonsense about marriage and women" which, she thought, could only have come from a "frightened bachelor"[2]), T.S. Eliot, Owen Barfield, J.R.R. Tolkien, and E.C. Bentley (another writer of superior detective fiction). She was much influenced by G.K. Chesterton whom she met in 1917, and of whom she wrote,

> To the young people of my generation, G.K.C. was a kind of Christian liberator. Like a beneficent bomb, he blew out of the Church a quantity of stained glass of a very poor period, and let in the gusts of fresh air in which the dead leaves of doctrine danced with all the energy and indecorum of Our Lady's Tumbler.[3]

In her later years she abandoned the detective genre and focused on writing about social and religious subjects. One of her best-known works was the cycle of radio plays, *The Man Born to be King*, broadcast on the BBC during the war. In her middle age Sayers got about the place on a motor-cycle. A minor planet, Sayers 3627, was named after her.

Our present purposes are best served by considering Sayers' work under four general headings: her theology, the general critique of contemporary society, then more particularly her views about the proper nature of work and the social position of women. She published more than a dozen books that were either exclusively or largely concerned with ecclesiastical and theological questions. The most influential of these were *Creed or Chaos? And Other Essays in Popular Theology* (1940) and *The Mind of the Maker* (1941). The first was an exposition, with an Anglo-Catholic coloring, of the fundamental Christian dogmas. C.S. Lewis's later book *Mere Christianity* (1952) was in rather the same manner, addressed to that mysterious entity, "the general reader," rather than to theologians and schol-ars—though both Lewis and Sayers could more than hold their own in such company. *The Mind of the Maker* constructed a model of human creativity inspired by the doctrine of the Trinity in which the hypostatic "three persons" are identified with the Idea (God), the Energy (Christ), and the Power (Holy Ghost). This, Sayers argued, furnished a model of the analogous creative literary pro-cess, corresponding to inspiration (invisibly present in the mind of the writer), the actual act of writing, and the meaning of the fin-ished product in the minds of readers. She approvingly quotes the Russian theologian Nikolai Berdayev:

> God created man in his own image and likeness, i.e., made him a creator too, calling him to free spontaneous activity and not to formal obedience to His power. Free creativeness is the creature's answer to the great call of its creator. Man's creative work is the fulfilment of the Creator's secret will.[4]

This idea was foundational in Sayers' understanding of work—about which more presently. Sayers hoped that *The Mind of the Maker* comprised a fertile interaction of literature and theology. It was well received and sympathetically reviewed, by C.S. Lewis amongst others.[5]

In her writings on Christianity Sayers focused on traditional doc-trines that, she insisted, comprised a rationally defensible response to all the Big Questions. She was irritated by people who thought of religion primarily in terms of feeling and behaving at the expense of thinking. Of herself she said, "I am quite without the thing known as 'inner light' or 'spiritual experience,'" laying claim rather to a "passionate intellect."[6] She was particularly severe on a weak-knee'd theological *laissez-faire*. Here she is unleashing one of her many fusillades:

> It is worse than useless for Christians to talk about the importance of Christian morality, unless they are prepared to take their stand upon the fundamentals of Christian theology. It is a lie to say that dogma does not matter; it matters enormously. It is fatal to let people suppose that Christianity is only a mode of feeling; it is vitally necessary to insist that it is first and foremost a rational

explanation of the universe. It is hopeless to offer Christianity as a vaguely idealistic aspiration of a simple and consoling kind; it is, on the contrary, a hard, tough, exacting, and complex doctrine, steeped in a drastic and uncompromising realism. And it is fatal to imagine that everybody knows quite well what Christianity is and needs only a little encouragement to practice it. The brutal fact is that in this Christian country not one person in a hundred has the faintest notion what the Church teaches about God or man or society or the person of Jesus Christ. . . . Theologically this country is at present in a state of utter chaos established in the name of religious toleration and rapidly degenerating into flight from reason and the death of hope.[7]

"Tolerance" was too often a cover for apathy and indifference, as she made clear in a biting statement about the nihilism so widespread in the "post-Christian" world:

In the world it is called Tolerance, but in hell it is called Despair . . . the sin that believes in nothing, cares for nothing, seeks to know nothing, interferes with nothing, enjoys nothing, hates nothing, finds purpose in nothing, lives for nothing, and remains alive because there is nothing for which it will die.[8]

Sayers was also a sharp critic of what Rowan Williams has called the "cosiness" (as mentioned earlier) of the Anglican Church, by which I surmise him to mean religion as a kind of social club, a matter of vicarage tea-parties, church fêtes, talks by furloughed missionaries, vestry meetings about the state of the hassocks, anodyne sermons, and a peculiarly English kind of fustiness . . . all brilliantly depicted, incidentally, in the gently satiric novels of Barbara Pym, Sayers' contemporary and fellow-writer. For Sayers the figure of Jesus was a confronting and "shattering personality" whom the Church had often reduced to a boring and tedious figure: "We have efficiently pared the claws of the Lion of Judah, certified him 'meek and mild,' and recommended him as a fitting household pet for pale curates and pious old ladies."[9] Nor did Sayers have much patience with the fashionable and uncritical acceptance of science as the arbiter of "reality":

> Why do you balk at the doctrine of the Trinity—God the three in One—yet meekly acquiesce when Einstein tells you E = mc²? What makes you suppose that the expression "God ordains" is narrow and bigoted, while your own expression, "Science demands" is taken as an objective statement of fact?

Sayers' view of post-war Britain, mediated by her reflections on Dante's portrayal of a diseased society, was not flattering. Here's what she saw:

> Futility; lack of a living faith; the drift into loose morality, greedy consumption, financial irresponsibility, and uncontrolled bad temper; a self-opinionated and obstinate individualism; violence, sterility, and lack of reverence for life and property . . . the exploitation of sex, the debasing of language . . . the commercializing of religion . . . mass hysteria and "spell-binding," venality and string-pulling in public affairs . . . the fomenting of discord . . . the exploitation of the lowest and stupidest mass-emotions. . . .[10]

Not hard to imagine how repulsed she would have been by the situation today in which most of these maladies of modernity now appear in even more extreme and grotesque forms. A visitor from Mars would only need a few hours in front of a television set, preferably tuned to Fox/Sky, to confirm the diagnosis.

Lest the reader be tempted, on the basis of the above excerpts, to suppose that Sayers was a forceful but rather grey and humorless social critic, it might be well to recall that she was also a writer of some grace, charm, and wit with a gift for the nicely turned phrase. Her plays and novels, as well as many of her essays, are redolent with such attractions:

> There's nothing you can't prove if your outlook is only sufficiently limited.

> "Do you find it easy to get drunk on words?" "So easy that, to tell you the truth, I am seldom perfectly sober."

> Some people's blameless lives are to blame for a good deal.

> The great advantage about telling the truth is that nobody ever believes it.

> He was so crooked you could have used his spine for a safety-pin.

A man was taken to the Zoo and shown the giraffe. After gazing at it a little in silence: "I don't believe it," he said.[11]

Sayers is also often attributed with the appealing maxim that "A woman fit to be a man's wife is too good to be his servant," but it seems that this belongs to Dorothy Leigh's work, *The Mother's Blessing*, 1616. Still, it *is* the sort of thing Dorothy Sayers might well have said. She certainly wouldn't disagree with the sentiment.

Much more might be said about Sayers as a critic of the contemporary world, but let's home in on two subjects close to her heart: the nature of work and the position of women. Her ideas about the former are signaled in her eloquent restatement of what was for centuries the accepted Christian view, and we might add, the same philosophy of work found in many different traditions, conspicuously in Platonism and in the Hindu tradition:

> Christians must revive a centuries-old view of humankind as made in the image of God, the eternal Craftsman, and of work as a source of fulfillment and blessing not as a necessary drudgery to be undergone for the purpose of making money, but as a way of life in which the nature of man should find its proper exercise and delight and so fulfill itself to the glory of God. That it should, in fact, be thought of as a creative activity undertaken for the love of the work itself; and that man, made in God's image, should make things, as God makes them, for the sake of doing well a thing that is well worth doing.[12]

Her critique of contemporary civilization is tied in with this view of work and continues a long tradition of anti-capitalist and anti-industrialist writings in England, stretching back to Blake and running through the Romantic poets and such figures as John Ruskin and William Morris. In a passage such as the following, Sayers is echoing many of her predecessors in a lineage that now includes writers like Kathleen Raine and my friend and colleague, the late Roger Sworder.[13]

> Unless we do change our whole way of thought about work, I do not think we shall ever escape from the appalling squirrel cage of economic confusion in which we have been madly turning for the last three centuries or so, the cage in which we landed ourselves by

acquiescing in a social system based upon Envy and Avarice. A society in which consumption has to be artificially stimulated in order to keep production going is a society founded on trash and waste, and such a society is a house built upon sand.

The essay *Why Work?* (from which these excerpts are taken) is the text of an address given in 1942. If I could only save one of Sayers' works for posterity, this would be it.

Finally, a few words about Sayers' stance on the position of women. Let's start with her acute observations about Jesus's dealings with women:

> Perhaps it is no wonder that the women were first at the Cradle and last at the Cross. They had never known a man like this Man—there never has been such another. A prophet and teacher who never nagged at them, never flattered or coaxed or patronized; who never made arch jokes about them, never treated them either as "The women, God help us!" or "The ladies, God bless them!"; who rebuked without querulousness and praised without condescension; who took their questions and arguments seriously; who never mapped out their sphere for them, never urged them to be feminine or jeered at them for being female; who had no axe to grind and no uneasy male dignity to defend; who took them as he found them and was completely unself-conscious. There is no act, no sermon, no parable in the whole Gospel that borrows its pungency from female perversity; nobody could possibly guess from the words and deeds of Jesus that there was anything "funny" about woman's nature.

In many respects Sayers might be seen as an outspoken and feisty feminist, historically situated in her mid-career between the "first wave" suffragettes and the "second wave" feminists of the late '60s and '70s. Certainly she did not hold back in her criticisms of what feminists now call the patriarchy and its many misogynistic manifestations. But Sayers herself did not like the term "feminist" and was at some pains to distance herself from such a label. Her general position is well-stated by one of her publishers:

> Sayers did not devote a great deal of time to talking or writing about feminism, but she did explicitly address the issue of women's role in society in the two classic essays collected here. Central to Sayers'

56

reflections is the conviction that both men and women are first of all human beings and must be regarded as essentially much more alike than different. We are to be true not so much to our sex as to our humanity. The proper role of both men and women, in her view, is to find the work for which they are suited and to do it.[14]

In the mischievously titled *Are Women Human?* she says this:

In reaction against the age-old slogan, "woman is the weaker vessel," or the still more offensive, "woman is a divine creature," we have, I think, allowed ourselves to drift into asserting that "a woman is as good as a man," without always pausing to think what exactly we mean by that. What, I feel, we ought to mean is something so obvious that it is apt to escape attention altogether, viz.: … that a woman is just as much an ordinary human being as a man, with the same individual preferences, and with just as much right to the tastes and preferences of an individual. *What is repugnant to every human being is to be reckoned always as a member of a class and not as an individual person* [italics mine].

Elsewhere in the same piece we find this:

When the pioneers of university training for women demanded that women should be admitted to the universities, the cry went up at once: "Why should women want to know about Aristotle?" The answer is NOT that all women would be the better for knowing about Aristotle ... but simply: "What women want as a class is irrelevant. I want to know about Aristotle. It is true that many women care nothing about him, and a great many male undergraduates turn pale and faint at the thought of him—but I, eccentric individual that I am, do want to know about Aristotle, and I submit that there is nothing in my shape or bodily functions which need prevent my knowing about him."

No doubt there are all sorts of arguments that might be mounted from a feminist point of view, both for and against Sayers' statement. Here is not the place to canvas them. What is notable in all of Sayers' writings on this subject is her insistence on the irreducible individuality of each person. She also dismissed such notions as the "the woman's point of view." Her response to requests from "congenital idiots and editors of magazines" to express such a view about the writing of detective fiction was this: "Go away and don't be silly. You might as well ask what is the female angle on an equilateral triangle." None of this should be construed to mean that she was indifferent to the collective plight of women, as her writings clearly testify. But ultimately her most profound concerns and her deepest pieties transcended all gender-related questions. She would not have approved of that facile slogan shouted in the streets of Paris in 1968, "Nothing outside politics."

Bede Griffiths

1906–1993

The Marriage of East and West

We begin to realize that truth is one, but that it has many faces, and each religion is, as it were, a face of the one Truth, which manifests itself under different signs and symbols in the different historical traditions.[1]

lan Griffiths was born into a middle-class Anglican family in 1906.[2] He exhibited a keen intellect at school and went on to studies at Oxford, where he belonged to the "Aesthetes" rather than the "Athletes," developing a life-long enthusiasm for Wordsworth and Coleridge, and for Romantic nature-mysticism. As a seventeen-year-old he experienced an epiphany while walking near his school's playing fields. He had suddenly felt himself to be in "the Garden of Paradise," and was overcome by a sense of awe: "I hardly dared look on the face of the sky, because it seemed as though it was but a veil before the face of God."[3] Nevertheless, he left Oxford with a vague agnosticism and, disenchanted with the modern world, went to live in austere simplicity with two friends in a small cottage in the Cotswolds. Through his studies there, his friendship with C.S. Lewis (who dedicated *Surprised by Joy* to Griffiths) and other "Inklings" such as Owen Barfield, and through several other formative experiences, his religious faith was awakened, leading him into the fold of the Roman Catholic Church and his eventual commitment to a monastic vocation. He was now convinced that "the rediscovery of religion is the great intellectual, moral, and spiritual adventure of our time."[4] In 1933 he entered the Benedictine Prinknash Abbey in Gloucester and was ordained to the priesthood in 1940. He served in various monastic roles. The story of Griffiths' early life and his conversion to Catholicism is told in his captivating spiritual autobiography, *The Golden String* (1954).

One of Carl Jung's earliest followers, Toni Sussman, had escaped from Germany with her Jewish husband and settled in London, where she opened a yoga and meditation center. It was partly under Sussman's influence that Griffiths' interest in the East was quickened in the early '40s, leading to intensive study of Eastern Scriptures from the Hindu, Buddhist, and Chinese traditions.[5] Griffiths left for India in 1955, "to seek for the other half of my soul."[6] He had received an invitation from an Indian Benedictine to establish a monastery in the Bangalore region, an enterprise that was never realized but which led to an encounter with Father Francis Mahieu, a Belgian Cistercian. Mahieu, a few years younger, had arrived in India with similar aspirations, a few months after the Englishman. The two monks established a Cistercian ashram, "Kurishumala," at Kottayam in Kerala. They followed the Syrian liturgy, which was deeply rooted in Kerala, tracing its origins back to the arrival of St Thomas the Apostle on the Malabar coast in AD 52. Kerala has long been the most Christian of the Indian states, something in the order of a third of its population being of this faith. Here Griffiths remained for ten years, serving as the novice master. In 1968 he was invited to take charge of another Christian ashram, Saccidananda, which had been established by Jules Monchanin and Henri Le Saux (now known as Swami Abhishiktananda). Monchanin was long since dead and Abhishiktananda had retired to his Himalayan hermitage. The latter's commitment to the ashram had always been somewhat ambivalent, the life of the solitary *sannyasi* always beckoning after his "shattering" experiences at Arunachala. (See the essay on Abhishiktananda.) Griffiths' arrival was to give the ashram a new lease of life; his presence was the key factor in attracting Indian monks of whom some fifteen were in permanent residence by the early '90s. The ashram also became a vibrant center for spiritual seekers from all over the globe, many attracted by the *darsan* (spiritual radiance) of Griffiths himself. He has sometimes been called "charismatic," which indeed he was, but not in the now colloquial sense of someone with flashy oratorical skills, a highly extrovert personality and the like: the qualities that struck many visitors, myself included, were his sweetness, gentleness, and natural courtesy combined with strength and fearlessness, as well as that sense of humor which is so often one of the marks of the wise.

The achievement was not without considerable personal cost to Griffiths himself: physical hardship, loneliness, illness, some personal tensions with Abhishiktananda, vitriolic attacks from evangelical fundamentalists, hostility from some Hindu quarters, difficulties with ecclesiastical authorities (some of whom were angered by Griffiths' bold calls for sweeping reforms within the Church and his stinging criticisms of Cardinal Ratzinger and other ecclesiastical heavyweights).[7] In his later years Griffiths became increasingly convinced that the authoritarian, highly bureaucratized, legalistic structures of the Church and its over-rationalized and masculinist doctrinal edifice must give way to a renewed mystical tradition. He remarked to Matthew Fox, "If Christianity cannot recover its mystical tradition and teach it, it should simply fold up and go out of business—it has nothing to offer."[8] He also observed, with characteristic insouciance, "Don't worry about the Vatican. It will all come tumbling down overnight someday, just like the Berlin Wall."[9]

In 1980 Father Bede formally joined the Camaldolese Order, under whose auspices the ashram thereafter operated. In his last years two strokes seem to have ignited further mystical illumination, much as Abhishiktananda's heart attack shortly before his death presaged "an extraordinary spiritual adventure."[10] We have the testimony of many who knew Griffiths in the last months of his life that he was filled, in St Benedict's phrase, with "the inexpressible sweetness of love."[11] Griffiths died in 1993 and was succeeded as prior by the Indian Brother Martin John Kuvarupu. By the time of his death Griffiths was widely known in the West and tributes were forthcoming from figures such as Cardinal Hume, the Dalai Lama, Andrew Harvey, Helen Luke, Yehudi Menuhin, Raimundo Panikkar, Matthew Fox, Odette Baumer-Despeigne, and many others. Griffiths' life story has been recounted in an intelligent, sympathetic, and unsentimental biography by Shirley du Boulay, *Beyond the Darkness: A Biography of Bede Griffiths* (1998).

The last two decades of Griffiths' life saw him travel widely in Europe, America, Asia, and Australia, lecturing, participating in conferences and retreats, meeting religious leaders such as the Dalai Lama. He was an indefatigable scholar and writer, producing some three hundred articles. His ten books found a responsive audience in the West and many were translated into other languages. Along with *The Golden String*, the most important were *Return to the Centre* (1976), *The Marriage of East and West* (1982), *The Cosmic Revelation: The Hindu Way to God* (1983), and *A New Vision of Reality: Western Science, Eastern Mysticism, and Christian Faith* (1989). Unlike Abhishiktananda, Griffiths took a close interest in intellectual and cultural developments in the West and, for better or worse, was more attuned to the contemporary spirit. In his later years, for instance, he avidly read the works of contemporary thinkers like Ken Wilber, Frithjof Capra, David Bohm, Matthew Fox, and Rupert

Sheldrake. Depending on one's point of view, one might either regret or applaud Griffiths' efforts to stay abreast of the latest developments in Western theology, philosophy, psychology, and physics, which, in his last book, he sought to synthesize with traditional Christian and Hindu doctrines and with the teachings of the mystics.

Wayne Teasdale has argued that Griffiths' life is best understood as a search for Wholeness, a goal to be reached through a synthesis of the values and modes of both East and West. In his pre-India days he had taken a close interest in the work of Jung and often returned to the great Jungian theme of the reconciliation of the opposites, particularly the masculine and the feminine. Like many pilgrims to the East, Griffiths was a resolute critic of those aspects of Western life that stifled spirituality—a hyper-rational and over-masculinized intellectual ethos that privileged conceptualization and analytical reason over intuition and direct experience, a life-style riddled with materialism and consumerism, the absence of any living sense of the sacred, the brutal desecration of Nature herself, the ossification of religious forms, the exclusivism, authoritarianism, and legalism of ecclesiastical institutions, the blind technological frenzy. He was by no means insensible to the achievements of Western culture and science, nor did he reject the Judeo-Christian moral heritage. Rather, he found in Indian spirituality and in the values and customs of traditional village life, an antidote to many of the ills that beset the West while always believing that the West had its own gifts to share with the East.

The "problem" of religious pluralism was less acute for Bede Griffiths than for his predecessors, largely because of the more hospitable climate engendered by Vatican II and by the conciliar document *Nostra Aetate* which radically modified both the exclusivism and the triumphalism of the Catholic Church in relation to other religions. We can trace in his writings a very clear trajectory from an early variant of fulfillment theology, through a period of uncertainty about the relationship of the world's major religions, arriving finally at a theology of religious diversity that is substantially the same as that of the perennialists and of neo-Hinduism, what has sometimes been called the complementarity theory—in brief, the idea that the seemingly divergent religions are different paths to the same summit.[12] Certainly, Father Bede believed that Christianity had a unique contribution to make to the world's spiritual treasury, and his own commitment to Christ never wavered. On the other hand he was victim to neither "fulfillment" nor "inclusivist" theology, each of which saw other religious traditions as somehow preparatory to Christianity. In the light of Griffiths' maturing understanding of the perennial philosophy, the problem of religious pluralism simply dissolved. As early as 1956, Griffiths had spoken and written of the timeless wisdom of which the religions are but particular expressions that have been corrupted, but that are *"divine in their origin"*: "they are all in their different ways forms of the one true religion, which has been made known to man from the beginning of the world"[13]—words that easily could have come from the pen of René Guénon.[14] In *The Marriage of East and West* Griffiths had written,

> It is no longer possible for one religion to live in isolation from other religions. For many this presents a real problem. Each religion has been taught to regard itself as the one true religion.... We begin to realize that truth is one, but that it has many faces, and each religion is, as it were, a face of the one Truth, which manifests itself under different signs and symbols in the different historical traditions.[15]

This is precisely one of the central principles of the traditionalist understanding of the *sophia perennis*. Echoing Abhishiktananda, Griffiths spoke of the renunciate's vocation to penetrate the world of religious forms in order to reach their formless essence:

> the *Sannyasi* is called to go beyond all religion, beyond every human institution, beyond every scripture and creed, till he comes to that which every religion and scripture and ritual signifies but can never name.

But the call to go "beyond all religion" could never mean the rejection of religion: "To go beyond the sign is not to reject the sign, but to reach the thing signified."[16] Griffiths remained alert to the dangers of both syncretism—the assembling of heterogeneous elements from different religions into a spurious unity—and a sentimental "universalism," a kind of religious "Esperanto" as Coomaraswamy called it, based on the absurd notion that the particular forms of each religion were now "out-dated."[17] Doubtless he would have endorsed Frithjof Schuon's remark,

> as for an exhausting of the religions, one might speak of this if all men had by now become saints or Buddhas. In that case only could it be admitted that the religions were exhausted, at least as regards their forms.[18]

Bede Griffiths has attracted some caustic criticism from traditionalists. Rama Coomaraswamy, for example, has lamented the influence on Griffiths' thought of Aurobindo and of Marxist and evolutionist ideas, and situates Griffiths, along with Mahesh Yogi, Aurobindo, and Bhagavan Rajneesh, in "the desacralisation of Hinduism for Western consumption."[19] There is no denying that Griffiths sometimes fell prey to modernistic and evolutionistic ideas. Nonetheless, in my view, Rama Coomaraswamy's judgement is harsh and fails to take into account the very considerable common ground that Griffiths shares with the traditionalists.

A Personal Reminiscence

I reached Shantivaman, in the small south Indian village of Tannirpali, after a long and riotous train and bus journey, completed on an ox-drawn cart. Here I joined in the daily life of worship, prayer, meditation, study, and work, and was twice able to have a lengthy conversation with Bede Griffiths, who was intensely interested in my account of perennialism and who at that point had no knowledge of the works of Guénon, Coomaraswamy, or Schuon. He had a particular interest in the tensions between what were thought of as "religion" and "science." Some years later I noticed an article in which Father Bede was discussing the work of Seyyed Hossein Nasr and his critique of modern scientism. Whether my enthusiasm for the perennialists had anything to do with his later reading I know not. I'm pleased to think that such a case was at least possible.

Father Bede was an arresting figure. Tall, vital, still physically attractive despite the encroachments of old age, which included a slight stoop. At this point he was 74, the same age as I am at the moment of writing. His long years in India had also given a certain Indian accent to his bearing and manner of speech though he also retained his unmistakable Englishness. He gave *satsang* each afternoon, a motley assortment of seekers and devotees from all over the world gathered at his feet. As well there were the other permanent residents in the ashram and a few folk from the local village. Father Bede would give a discourse on some religious theme, after which there would be questions and discussion. He was softly spoken, very articulate, gentle in demeanor, and radiating what the Buddhists would call *prajna* and *karuna*, compassionate wisdom. Certainly one of the most impressive and saintly persons I've had the good fortune to meet in this lifetime. Despite the radical differences between them he reminded me in some ways of Lama Zopa at whose feet I had sat some years earlier, during a Buddhist *lam-rin* retreat at the Chenrezig Institute in Queensland.

In the early morning and at dusk we worshipped in a beautiful small chapel that Father Bede had designed himself, following an ancient Syrian Christian liturgy but leavened with readings from the Scriptures of the East. The chanting and singing at the evening services was beautiful—evocative, soul-stirring, almost celestial. When we weren't engaged in worship, meditation, or *satsang* we completed a few simple chores in the kitchen or garden, wandered through the palms and eucalypts along the banks of the Kavery river, where one espied cattle bathing in the river, women doing their laundry, urchins at play. I also spent a lot of time in the library, another lovely building Father Bede had designed and helped to build. It was well stocked, an assortment of books being left behind by the many wayfarers who had stopped over at the ashram. All in all it was a magical, inspiring, and purifying week.

Simone Weil

1909–1943

Paying Attention

*There is not any department of human life
which is purely natural. The supernatural is
secretly present throughout.*[1]

imone Weil is one of those arresting figures, few in any age, who defy all categorizations but who seem in some sense to dramatize the peculiar conditions of the time in which they live—in her case conditions of unprecedented spiritual sterility, social dislocation, and political barbarism. But, somewhat paradoxically, it is the uniqueness of such persons, their singular nature, that enables them to feel the pulse of the times in which they live. A radical estrangement from the cultural milieu seems to endow them with a kind of second sight. I suggested earlier that in the nineteenth century Dostoevsky, Nietzsche, and Kierkegaard were such figures, all, like Weil, thinkers of the most intense and unflinching seriousness. As one commentator has recently observed, perhaps she is worth reading today "precisely because her tone is so alien, yet her concerns still so contemporary."[2] Almost everything about her—her life, personality, and character, her thought and writing, her religious orientation and spiritual life, even the manner of her death, is exceptional. She is one of the most admired and least understood of modern religious thinkers, one quite without "followers," her sensibility and experience altogether beyond any kind of "imitation." André Gide hailed Weil as "the patron saint of all outsiders" and "the most truly spiritual writer of this century." Susan Sontag refers to her "scathing originality." Albert Camus described her as "*the* one great spirit of our times." Weil has been approached from many different angles, labeled with all manner of terms, often quite contradictory ones. Rebel, outsider, teacher, existentialist, philosopher, activist, prophet, anarchist, mystic, martyr, heretic, neurotic, anti-Semite, madwoman. Even the most poised and erudite of culture critics, George Steiner most notably, have been thrown off balance by Weil.[3] An enigma, a scandal, an inspiration. Interest in her shows no signs of abating. A recent "meta study" (whatever that might be!) revealed that between 1995 and 2012 over 2,500 new scholarly works about her had been published. Good luck with the literature review! From among the many public intellectuals, artists, and religious who have paid her eloquent tribute we may select a sample: T.S. Eliot, Pope Paul VI, Thomas Merton, Hannah Arendt, Emil Cioran, Maurice Blanchot, Giorgio Agamben, Rowan Williams,

Nicola Chiaromonte, Czeslaw Milosz—all from the heavyweight division!

A figure of such perplexing originality, of "multiple spiritual complexities,"[4] poses a daunting challenge to any overview let alone a comprehensive account of her contribution to modern thought. No such agenda here. Instead, a quick sketch of her short life and some remarks about three aspects of her thought: her diagnosis of contemporary political maladies and maledictions, particularly her thinking about two now highly problematic terms, "justice" and "rights"; her understanding of prayer; her decision to remain outside the Catholic Church.

Weil was born in Paris into a comfortable middle-class family of secularized and agnostic Jews.[5] From a very young age she displayed precocious and prodigious intellectual talents. As a child during the Great War she refused to eat sugar because the soldiers at the front had none; this identification with those who were suffering—workers, soldiers, prisoners, exiles, refugees—became a motif in her life, and indeed, her death. Among her early enthusiasms were the ancient Greek language, Plato, Sanskrit, The *Bhagavad Gita*. She studied philosophy at the École Normale Supérieure after taking first place in the entrance exam in Philosophy and Logic (Simone de Beauvoir came second). Her classmates at university were disconcerted by her fierce intelligence, her independence of mind. and her passionate political convictions as well as her apparent erasure of her own sexuality, nicknaming her "The Martian" and "The Red Virgin." She was "a spectacularly impractical person who lived most of her life on a level of abstraction and absent-mindedness."[6]

Weil taught philosophy at a secondary girls' school while hurling herself into political activism on behalf of the French working class, with whom she closely identified herself. At this point she could fairly be described as a pacifist, Marxist, and trade unionist. Her emerging social and political philosophy revolved around the nature of power, freedom, and justice, and the spectres of mass dehumanization and totalitarianism of both a technological and ideological kind. She was also deeply engaged with questions about the nature of work, arguing in one of her essays that a civilization could only achieve greatness when it was founded on "the spirituality of work."

In 1936 she joined the Republican forces in Spain where she displayed a total ineptitude for combat of any kind, struggling to distinguish one end of a rifle from the other. After a few weeks with the Durutti Column anarchists, while cooking, she badly burnt herself (she was notoriously clumsy) and had to be rescued by her family. She was taken, perhaps providentially, to Assisi to recover. There she had an ecstatic religious experience that provoked her into falling to her knees in prayer for the first time in her life. Attending Easter services, she wrote, "the Passion of Christ entered into my being once and for all" and thereafter "the name of God and the name of Christ [were] irresistibly mingled with my thoughts."[7] A year after her Assisi experience she had another transformative illumination in which, she said, "Christ himself came down and took possession of me."[8] From this point onwards, without ever surrendering her involvement in social and political issues, her concerns became ever more deeply philosophical, religious, and mystical. She was profoundly attracted to the Catholic tradition but declined to be baptized.

During WWII Weil lived in Marseilles, traveled to the USA, and involved herself in the French Resistance movement in England. She suffered ill-health throughout her life, was afflicted with tuberculosis in England, and died from a cardiac arrest in a sanatorium in Kent. During the last weeks of her life she had eaten almost nothing. The circumstances and precise cause of her death, her psychological state, her motivations in refusing food and treatment, have all been debated ever since. But there is no doubt that her self-naughting identification with the victims of war was a cooperative cause in her demise. One of her biographers concluded, "As to her death, whatever explanation one may give of it will amount in the end to saying that she died of love."[9]

Many who knew Weil, and indeed, many later commentators, were alarmed by "her contempt for pleasure and for happiness, her noble and ridiculous political gestures, her elaborate self-denials, her tireless courting of affliction."[10] Her own brother, the distinguished mathematician André Weil, observed that "her sensibility had gone beyond the limits of the normal." Much has been made of this by those wanting to argue, with George Steiner, that both her thinking and her behavior "lie at the shadow-line of the pathological." Without descending into this quagmire of controversy it might be noted that André Weil's observation is amenable to quite contradictory inflections; it is usually mobilized to support the case that Simone was "mad," "deranged," "pathological," but it might also be accented in quite a different way. In her experience, her behavior, and her thinking, Weil undoubtedly went "beyond the limits of the normal"; but the same could be said of countless mystics, saints and sages!

Throughout her adult life Weil wrote voluminously—essays, tracts, reviews, pamphlets, letters, notebooks—but never published a book. Her writings were assembled in several posthumous compilations, the most influential being *Gravity and Grace* and *Waiting for God*. Since her death various collections and anthologies of her writings have been published, including *The Notebooks of Simone Weil*. Her thinking often proceeds through paradoxes. In her notebooks she jotted, "Method of investigation—as soon as one has arrived at a position, try to find in what sense the contrary is true."[11] She also had a gift for the *aperçu*, the aphorism, the elegantly turned maxim. Before turning to our main concerns let me share a few of my favorites, each one suggestive of a recurrent theme:[12]

> The beautiful is the experimental proof that the incarnation is possible.

> Imaginary evil is romantic and varied; real evil is gloomy, monotonous, barren, boring. Imaginary good is boring; real good is always new, marvelous, intoxicating.

> The mysteries of faith are degraded if they are made into an object of affirmation and negation, when in reality they should be an object of contemplation.

> The danger is not that the soul should doubt whether there is any bread, but that, by a lie, it should persuade itself that it is not hungry.

> Money, mechanization, algebra. The three monsters of contemporary civilization.

> Official history is a matter of believing murderers on their own word.

Fortunately the sky is beautiful everywhere.

The effective part of the will is not effort . . . it is consent.

There is something mysterious in the universe which is in complicity with those who desire nothing but the good.

One has only the choice between God and idolatry. There is no other possibility. For the faculty of worship is in us, and it is either directed somewhere into this world, or into another.

Now to the three issues flagged earlier: the political pathologies of the time; the nature of prayer; religious conversion. Even at the height of her Marxist fervor Weil did not become a member of the Communist Party: she was not a joiner. She was ferociously opposed to "groupthink" of any kind: "The intelligence is defeated as soon as the expression of one's thought is preceded, explicitly or implicitly, by the little word 'we.'"[13] She was deeply suspicious of the apparatus of the State and of *all* political parties, arguing that they were driven by three malign purposes: to generate collective passions, to exert collective pressure on individuals, and to perpetuate their own existence. Her writings vibrate with sharp political insights no less pertinent today than in those darkened days in Europe. For instance: "A democracy where public life is made up of strife between political parties is incapable of preventing the formation of a party whose avowed aim is the overthrow of that democracy."[14] In *On the Abolition of All Political Parties*, written shortly before her death, this:

> Nearly everywhere—often even when dealing with purely technical problems—instead of thinking, one merely takes sides: for or against. Such a choice replaces the activity of the mind. This is an intellectual leprosy; it originated in the political world and then spread through the land, contaminating all forms of thinking. This leprosy is killing us.[15]

In *Gravity and Grace* Weil posited two powers in life in a kind of permanent dialectic, one ("gravity") a purely worldly force that fuels the pursuit of self-interest, the other ("grace") a supernatural source of good without which humankind is captive to "an extraordinarily complicated tangle of guerrilla forces" in which the competition for power may, on the social plane, bring about a certain equilibrium, a balance of conflicting forces in which "natural justice" (temporary and precarious) may sometimes be achieved. But, Weil argues, this kind of justice is not enough: supernatural justice, issuing from grace, entails an attentive respect for and love of the full humanity of every individual person, a love which calls on us

> to empty ourselves of our false divinity, to deny ourselves, to give up being the centre of the world in imagination, to discern that all points in the world are equally centres, and that the true centre is outside the world. . . .[16]

This is quite a different matter from asserting "rights," though these have their proper but subordinate place. As Weil tersely remarks somewhere, "One cannot imagine St Francis of Assisi talking about 'rights.'" Elsewhere she elaborates her misgivings about "rights" as a possible engine of social reform:

> If you say to someone who has ears to hear, "What you are doing to me is not just," you may touch and awaken at its source the spirit of attention and love. But it is not the same with words like "I have the right to..." or "you have no right to..." They evoke a latent war and awaken the spirit of contention. To place the notion of rights at the centre of social conflicts is to inhibit any possible impulse of charity on both sides.... Thanks to this word ["rights"], what should have been a cry of protest from the depth of the heart has been turned into a shrill nagging of claims and counter-claims, which is both impure and impractical.[17]

How appalled she would have been by the contemporary maelstrom of polarizing and totalizing rhetoric that now engulfs many discussions of "rights." The "spirit of attention and love," on the other hand, can only issue from grace. And so it is that "To treat our neighbor who is in affliction with love is something like baptizing him." Love of this kind is a reverberation of the Divine, manifested in generosity and compassion which, in the Christian context, have their "model in God," in the Creation, and in the Passion of Christ. "Attention is the rarest and purest form of generosity." Before we know God directly and lose ourselves in His love, we can experience intimations of it in our own disinterested love of our neighbor, of the natural world, and of religious ceremonies. In each case it is "God in us" who is the source of this love.

"Attention," a keynote in Weil's thought, is also at the center of her ideas about prayer which, in its highest reaches, is contemplation, a special kind of attention:

> Attention, taken to its highest degree, is the same thing as prayer. It presupposes faith and love. Absolutely unmixed attention is prayer. If we turn our mind toward the good, it is impossible that little by little the whole soul will not be attracted thereto in spite of itself.[18]

Rilke called prayer "a direction of the heart," a formulation rather different, at least on the face of it, from Weil's insistence that it is not a matter of generating and arranging "feeling," what she calls "warmth of heart," but of developing a kind of "emptiness," an "unselfing" that opens us to the workings of grace, a contemplative stillness and silence signaled by the title of one of her books, *Waiting for God*. The reference to "emptiness" might remind us that Weil was familiar with many Eastern doctrines and practices that may account for certain Zen-like resonances and a certain Buddhist aroma in her writings, as, for instance, here: "We have to be nothing in order to be in our right place in the whole," or "The renunciation of past and future is the first of all renunciations," or "A mind enclosed in language is in prison." Weil was also influenced by Pure Land Buddhism, in which the invocation of the Name of Amida Buddha is the path to salvation. In *Waiting for God* she writes that "Every religious practice, every rite, every liturgy is a form of the recitation of the name of the Lord, and must in principle really have virtue, the virtue of saving anyone devoted to it with desire."[19] In any event we may affirm certain affinities between Weil's thought and Eastern wisdom in its many forms.

Weil's writings on metaphysics, mysticism, and religion have generated a veritable industry of commentary, explication, and controversy, which we will by-pass. Her own spiritual trajectory and the nature of her mystical experiences are far too complex to unravel here. Much discussion of Weil is clouded by a failure to understand that, in the words of Mark Stone, "Weil was first and foremost a mystic, and all the power, authority and universality in her writing proceed from this fact."[20] Here we confine ourselves to a single question: why did Weil, despite the powerful attraction she felt to the Catholic Church and her spiritually intimate relationship with Father Perrin, decline to be baptized? There are several answers to this apparently simple question. One was adumbrated earlier: she was deeply suspicious of groups and institutions of all kinds, a perpetual outsider. She was, she said, afraid of being overwhelmed by "Church patriotism." She identified with all those who had been and were outside the fold of the Church:

> So many things are outside [the Church]. So many things that I love and do not want to give up, so many things that God loves, otherwise they would not be in existence. All the immense stretches of past centuries, except the last twenty, are among them; all the countries inhabited by colored races; all secular life in white countries; in the history of these countries, all the traditions banned as heretical. . . . Christianity being Catholic by right but not in fact, I regard it as legitimate on my part to be a member of the Church by right but not in fact, not only for a time, but for my whole life if need be.[21]

She was particularly troubled by the Church's use of "collective force" (always abhorrent to Weil) to exclude troublesome and nonconforming individuals from the sacrament and therefore from salvation. In a letter to Father Perrin she identifies "an *absolutely insurmountable* barrier" to her own formal entry into the Church:

> It is the use of two little words anathema sit. It is not their existence but the way they have been employed up till now. It is that also which prevents me from crossing the threshold of the Church. I remain beside all those things that cannot enter the Church, the universal repository, on account of those two little words.[22]

Related to this stance was Weil's posture on the question of religious conversion:

> If one is born into a religion that is not too unsuitable for pronouncing the name of the Lord, when one loves that native religion, well-oriented and pure, it is difficult to conceive of a legitimate motive to abandon it before direct contact with God

offers the soul to the divine will itself. Beyond this threshold, the change is only legitimate as an act of obedience. In fact history shows how this rarely happens. More often—perhaps always—the soul that reaches the highest spiritual regions is confirmed in the love of the tradition that served as its ladder. . . . [T]o change religions is an extremely grave decision and it is even more serious to push someone else to do so. It is still an infinitely more serious exercise, in this sense, to officially apply such pressure upon conquered lands.[23]

This passage raises the volatile question of Weil's relationship to the tradition into which she was born and, in the words of Rowan Williams, "her staggering insensitivity about Judaism, about which she wrote with hostility and incomprehension, as if her own Jewish identity was another embarrassing bit of particularity that needed to be abolished."[24] George Steiner, one of the most searching and discomforting of Weil's critics, has pressed the charge: "In Weil's detestation of her own ethnic identity . . . the traits of a classical Jewish self-loathing are carried to fever pitch. . . . Worst of all . . . is her refusal to envisage, in the midst of her eloquent pathos in respect of suffering and injustice, the horrors, the anathema being enacted on her own people."[25] This grave censure comes in the context of Steiner's carefully argued critique of other aspects of Weil's thought and his forensic exposure of a good deal of muddled commentary about her.[26] However, it should also be pointed out that Steiner finds much to admire in her writings. After some approbations of the work of Simone de Beauvoir and Hannah Arendt, he concludes his essay with this tribute, as well as taking a closing swipe at those who have "beatified" her: "But of the great feminine spirits abroad, that of Weil does strike one as the most evidently philosophic, as the most at home in the 'mountain light' (as Nietzsche would have it) of speculative abstraction. In that cold air, incense is out of place."[27]

Implicit in Weil's reflections about conversion we can discern another idea or principle that informed much of her writing and partially accounted for her refusal to "cross the threshold": religious universalism, the notion that all religious traditions offer a pathway to God. Ultimately, for Weil, all that matters is the journey of the soul towards God, or, as she sometimes calls the transcendent Reality, "the impersonal." Whatever might be conducive to that journey, both within and without Christianity, was from God; whatever impeded it derived entirely from the world of "gravity," from worldly forces that might be more or less benign, morally neutral, or evil, but that must be transcended if we are to find our full humanity. It is in this context that we should understand some of her "marvelously intemperate" declarations, such as "a science which does not take us closer to God is worthless."[28] Knowledge of God, to be attained through affliction and love, is the proper end of all human endeavor. Everyone "who has once touched the level of the impersonal is charged with a responsibility towards all human beings; to safeguard, not their persons, but whatever frail potentialities are hidden within them for passing over to the impersonal."[29]

Swami Abhishiktananda[1]

(Henri Le Saux)
1910–1973

With some notes
on Father Jules Monchanin
(1895–1957)

Christian-Hindu Encounter
and the Monastic Vocation

*The monk is a man who lives in the solitude of God, alone in
the very aloneness of the Alone… He does not become a monk in
order to do social work or intellectual work or missionary work or
to save the world. The monk simply consecrates himself to God.*[2]

Notes on Fr Jules Monchanin

y way of understanding the background to Swami Abhishiktananda's life and work in India it will be helpful to start with a quick sketch of his fellow-countryman Jules Monchanin, with whom he formed one of the earliest of the Christian ashrams in India. The first forty years of Monchanin's life were unexceptional for a provincial French priest.[3] He was born near Lyons in 1895, entered the priesthood as a young man, and completed his theological training in 1922. Despite his formidable intellectual gifts he did not complete his doctoral studies but instead asked to be sent to a miners' parish in a poor suburb of Lyons, later working as a chaplain. Since boyhood he had felt an attraction to India, which now steered him towards Sanskrit, and Indological and comparative religious studies. From the early '30s Monchanin was exploring the possibility of living some sort of Christian monastic life in India, no easy task for someone bound to Mother Church. It took many years of negotiations before he finally received the approval of the Bishop of Tiruchirapalli to work among the scattered Indian Christians in the region evangelized centuries before by Francis Xavier and Roberto Nobili. Monchanin left Marseilles for India in May 1939.

For the next decade Monchanin was immersed in pastoral work in southern India. These were years of social deprivation, physical hardship, and acute loneliness, preparatory to the contemplative life for which he yearned. In 1950 he was at last able to establish a monastic hermitage on the banks of the Kavery River, a Christian ashram that he and his fellow Benedictine and compatriot, Henri le Saux, called "Saccidananda." Le Saux articulated their agenda:

> Our goal: to form the first nucleus of a monastery (or rather a *laura*, a grouping of neighboring anchorites like the ancient *laura* of Saint Sabas in Palestine) that buttresses the Rule of Saint Benedict—a primitive, sober, discrete rule. Only one purpose: to seek God. And the monastery will be Indian style. We would like to crystalize and transubstantiate the search of the Hindu *sannyasi*. Advaita and the praise of the Trinity are our only aim. This means

we must grasp the authentic Hindu search for God in order to Christianize it, starting with ourselves first of all, from within.[4]

Vedantic philosophy, Christian theology, Indian lifestyle. The hope was that "what is deepest in Christianity may be grafted on to what is deepest in India." This was not a syncretic exercise that would issue forth some religious hybrid, but an attempt to fathom the depths of Christianity with the aid of the traditional wisdom of India which, in the monks' view, was to be found in Vedanta and the spiritual disciplines of the renunciate. The lifestyle was to be thoroughly Indian: meditation, prayer, study of the Scriptures of both traditions, a simple vegetarian diet, the most Spartan of amenities. Each donned the ochre cloth of the *sannyasi*, and took on the names of Arubianandam and Abhishiktananda.

Monchanin had alluded earlier to the case of Dom Joliet, a French naval officer in China who became a Benedictine in 1897 and waited thirty years to realize his dream of founding a Christian monastery in the Far East. Monchanin had written, "Will I someday know the same joy, that in India too—from its soil and spirit—there will come a [Christian] monastic life dedicated to contemplation?"[5] The dream was not to be fully realized in Monchanin's lifetime. On the face of it, the efforts of the French monks were less than successful: it was a constant struggle to keep the ashram afloat; there was little enthusiasm from either the European or Indian hierarchy; there were endless difficulties and hardships; not a single Indian monk became a permanent member of the ashram. By the time of Monchanin's death in 1957 there seemed little to show for the hard years behind them. But the seeds had been sown. A decade after Monchanin's death, Father Bede Griffiths and two Indian monks left their own southern Indian ashram and committed themselves to Saccidananda. There were many difficult years ahead, but Monchanin's dream finally came to fruition under Bede Griffiths.

In Monchanin we find a sharp intellect, considerable erudition, and a refined sensibility with an appreciation of Europe's cultural heritage; he might easily have fashioned a splendid academic or ecclesiastical career. In Le Saux's words, "He was one of the most brilliant intellects among the French clergy, a remarkable conversationalist, at home on every subject, a brilliant lecturer, and a theologian who opened before his hearers marvelous and ever new horizons."[6] Instead, all is surrendered to plunge himself into the materially impoverished life of the Indian villager and the eremitic life of the monk, the Christian *sannyasi*. In 1941 he had written in his journal, "May India take me and bury me within itself—in God."[7] It was a noble ideal.

The annals of Christian missionizing are replete with stories of heroic self-sacrifice, of dedication to tireless, often thankless work in arid fields, an exacting and lonely life in the service of Christian ideals—precisely, the pursuit of a vocation. Monchanin, however, is a fascinating case because in him the missionary dilemma, if one may so express it, becomes fully and acutely self-conscious. The poignancy and tragedy of Monchanin's life in India is that he was unable to find his way out of the dilemma. It is clear from his writings that he intuitively understood "the limits of religious expansionism" (to borrow a phrase from Frithjof Schuon). He was intelligent enough to see that insofar as Christians were bent on converting Indians, the enterprise was doomed to failure (the odd individual convert being the exception that proves the rule). He sensed that devout Hindus found the idea of conversion abhorrent, "a betrayal, cowardice." Shortly before his death he wrote,

> The root of the matter is that Hindus are not spiritually uneasy. They believe they possess supreme wisdom and thus how could they attach any importance to the fluctuations or investigations of those who possess lesser wisdom. Christ is one among *avataras*. Christianity in their eyes is a perfect moral doctrine, but a metaphysics that stops on the threshold of the ultimate metamorphosis.[8]

He was well-equipped to appreciate the vast storehouse of Indian spirituality. But throughout his life he felt bound to the conventional Christian belief in the ultimate superiority of his own faith, a position to which he was theologically committed by the weight of the centuries. His friend Père Henri de Lubac had characterized Monchanin's task this way: "to rethink everything in the light of theology, and to rethink theology through mysticism."[9] The problem was that the theology and the mysticism were pulling in opposite directions, the tension arising out of a dogmatic literalism and an ossified exotericism in the Catholic Church, which insisted on the *exclusive* truths of Christianity and, *ipso facto*, on its *superiority* to other faiths. During a near-fatal illness in 1932 Monchanin had vowed that, if he were to recover, he would devote himself to the salvation of India: his years in India taught him, at least subconsciously, that India, insofar as it still cleaved to Hindu orthodoxy, was in no need of salvation! Consider a few quotes from Monchanin's writings:

> India has stood for three millennia, if not longer, as the seat of one of the principal civilizations of mankind, equal to if not greater than that of Europe and China.... India has received from the Almighty an uncommon gift, an unquenchable thirst for whatever is spiritual. Since the time of the Vedas and the *Upanishads*, countless numbers of its sons have been great seekers of God.... Century after century there rose up seers and poets singing the joys and sorrows of a soul in quest of the One, and philosophers reminding every man of the supremacy of contemplation....

Cheek by jowl with lofty passages such as these we find quite contradictory ones:

> Unfortunately, Indian wisdom is tainted with erroneous tendencies.... Outside the unique revelation and the unique Church man is always and everywhere incapable of sifting truth from falsehood and good from evil.... So also, confident in the indefectible guidance of the Church, we hope that India, once baptized into the fullness of its body and soul and into the depth of its age-long quest for Brahma, will reject its pantheistic tendencies and, discovering in the splendors of the Holy Spirit the true mysticism and finding at last the vainly longed-for philosophical and theological equilibrium between antagonistic trends of thought, will bring forth for the good of humanity and the Church and ultimately for the glory of God unparalleled galaxies of saints and doctors ... we cannot hide [Hinduism's] fundamental error and its essential divergence in terms of Christianity. Hinduism must reject its *atman-brahman* equation, if it is to enter into Christ.[10]

The tensions between a rigid Christian exclusivism and a recognition of the spiritual depths of Hinduism could hardly be more apparent. Monchanin's life would have been much easier had the

Vatican II renovation of Catholic attitudes to other religions taken place half a century earlier. (Vatican II was, in common parlance, a "a very mixed bag," but the mitigation of centuries of exclusivism was a significant step in the right direction.) He might also have been spared much agonizing by recourse to the works of tradition-alists such as his fellow countryman, René Guénon. Seyyed Hossein Nasr states the problem concisely:

> The essential problem that the study of religion poses is how to preserve religious truth, traditional orthodoxy, the dogmatic theo-logical structures of one's own tradition, and yet gain knowledge of other traditions and accept them as spiritually valid ways and roads to God.[11]

This was the problem Monchanin could never resolve. His successor, Bede Griffiths, was able at least partially to resolve the dilemma by discerning that the task at hand was not to "Christianize" Hinduism—an undertaking to which the Indians themselves remained, for the most part, supremely indifferent—but to "Hinduize" Christianity, that is, to recover the mystical dimension of the Christian tradition and its metaphysical underpinnings by recourse to a sapiential wisdom and a more or less intact spiritual methodology still comparatively untouched by the ravages of modernity. This became the governing impulse of Griffiths' life and work.

Abhishiktananda

Henri Le Saux arrived in India in 1948 to join Monchanin in the monastic venture at Shantivanam. He was never to leave the shores of his adopted country. Le Saux was born in Brittany in 1910 and entered a Benedictine monastery in 1929. Like Monchanin, he felt the call of India as a young man but he too had to endure a lengthy wait before embarking for the sub-continent and achieving "his most ardent desire." Soon after setting up the modest ashram the two Benedictines traveled to Arunachala to visit the saintly Ramana Maharshi, who made the most profound impression on Le Saux:

> Even before my mind was able to recognize the fact, and still less to express it, the invisible halo of this Sage had been perceived by something in me deeper than any words. Unknown harmonies

awoke in my heart. . . . In the Sage of Arunachala of our time I discerned the Unique Sage of the eternal India, the unbroken succes-
sion of her sages, her ascetics, her seers; it was as if the very soul of
India penetrated to the very depths of my own soul and held mysterious communion with it. It was a call that pierced through
everything, rent it in pieces and opened a mighty abyss. . . .[12]

Frithjof Schuon gives a strikingly similar account of the Maharishi's
nature and significance:

In Sri Ramana Maharshi one meets again ancient and eternal
India. The Vedantic truth—the truth of the *Upanishads*—is
brought back to its simplest expression, but without any kind of
betrayal. . . . Sri Ramana was as it were the incarnation, in these
latter days and in the face of modern activist fever, of what is primordial and incorruptible in India. He manifested the nobility of
contemplative "non-action" in the face of an ethic of utilitarian
agitation and he showed the implacable beauty of pure truth in
the face of passions, weaknesses, and betrayals.[13]

In the years following Ramana's death, Le Saux spent two extended
periods as a hermit in one of the holy mountain's many caves. He
wrote of an overwhelming mystical experience while in retreat there
and stated that he was "truly reborn at Arunachala under the guidance of the Maharishi," understanding "what is beyond silence: *sun-
yata.*"[14] "Ramana's *Advaita* is my birthplace. Against that, all ration-
alization is shattered."[15] The French monk also became a disciple of
Sri Gnanananda Giri of Tiruykoyilur, giving an account of this in
Guru and Disciple (1967) and *The Secret of Arunachala* (1974). He
remarks that upon meeting Gnanananda he *automatically* yielded
his allegiance to him, something he had never previously done.[16]

Over the next few years Abhishiktananda gradually loosened his
connections with the ashram at Shantivanam (though he continued
to visit right up to the time of his death) and spent much of his time
as a wandering itinerant in the Himalayas. It was his impregnable
conviction that the life of renunciation was the meeting point of
Christianity and Hinduism:

Believe me, it is above all in the mystery of *sannyasa* that India and
the Church will meet, will discover themselves in the most secret

and hidden parts of their hearts, in the place where they are each most truly themselves, in the mystery of their origin in which every outward manifestation is rooted and from which time unfolds itself.[17]

He formalized his Indian citizenship in 1960—he had long been a spiritual citizen—and established a small hermitage on the banks of the Ganges at Uttarkashi in the Himalayas. Here he plunged ever deeper into the *Upanishads*, realizing more and more the Church's need of India's timeless message. He also consolidated his grasp of Sanskrit, Tamil, and English, and often participated in retreats, conferences, and interfaith gatherings. It was appropriate that most of his books were written here, near the source of the Ganges. In his last two years he gathered a small group of disciples. Abhishiktananda died in 1973. In his final illness he had experienced again "an inner apocalypse," "an awakening beyond all myths and symbols,"[18] returning him to one of his favorite Upanishadic verses (of which we can find echoes in many mystical works of both East and West):

> I know him, that great Purusha
> Of the colour of the sun,
> Beyond all darkness.
> He who has known him
> Goes beyond death.
> There is no other way.
> (*Svetasvatara Upanishad*, III.8.)

He wrote in one of his last letters, "the quest is fulfilled."

Abhishiktananda seems to have had a more natural affinity for the actual practices of Hindu spirituality than did Monchanin and was less troubled by the doctrinal tensions between the two traditions he was seeking to bridge. It is surely significant that it was Abhishiktananda who was able to surrender to the extraordinary *darsan* of Ramana. It is also suggestive that, of the three Benedictines associated with Saccidananda Ashram, only Le Saux became universally known under his Indian name. Unlike Monchanin, he became the *chela* of a Hindu guru, and was at home in the pilgrimage sites, the monasteries, and ashrams of India, mixing freely with swamis and sadhus the length and breadth of the subcontinent. One also gets the impression, in reading their more intimate letters and journals, that Abhishiktananda suffers little of Monchanin's angst about their missionizing. He makes an interesting contrast with Monchanin insofar as he gave *primacy to his own mystical realization* over the theological doctrines to which he was formally committed as a Christian. As he somewhere remarked, "Truth has to be taken from wherever it comes; that Truth possesses us—we do not possess Truth." On the basis of his own testimony and that of those who knew him in later years we can say that, through the penetration of religious forms, Abhishiktananda became a fully realized *sannyasi*, which is to say, neither Hindu nor Christian, or, if one prefers, both Christian and Hindu, this only being possible at a mystical level where the relative forms are universalized. As he wrote in *The Further Shore*, "The call to complete renunciation cuts across all dharmas and disregards all frontiers... it is anterior to every religious formulation."[19] One of his disciples referred to his "glorious transfiguration" and "the transparence of his whole being to the inner Mystery, the divine Presence."[20]

The fact that this kind of language is used indiscriminately about all manner of dubious "gurus" should not blind us to the fact that, in some cases—and this is one—such language is perfectly appropriate. In his diary, Abhishiktananda wrote of himself as "at once so deeply Christian and so deeply Hindu, at a depth where Christian and Hindu in their social and mental structures are blown to pieces, and are yet found again ineffably at the heart of each other."[21] As Frithjof Schuon has remarked,

> When a man seeks to escape from "dogmatic narrowness" it is essential that it should be "upwards" and not "downwards": dogmatic form is transcended by fathoming its depths and contemplating its universal content, and not by denying it in the name of a pretentious and iconoclastic "ideal" of "pure truth."[22]

Abhishiktananda never denied or repudiated the doctrines or practices of either Christianity or Hinduism, nor did he cease to observe the Christian forms of worship and to celebrate the sacraments; rather, he came to understand their limitations as religious *forms*, a form necessarily being limited by definition. His own "statements" on doctrinal matters, he said, were to be regarded as "no more than working hypotheses" and as "vectors of free inquiry."[23] Religious structures (doctrines, rituals, laws, and the like) were *signposts* to the Absolute but could not be invested with any absolute value in themselves. In this insight he again echoes Schuon who writes:

> Exotericism consists in identifying transcendent realities with the dogmatic forms, and if need be, with the historical facts of a given Revelation, whereas esotericism refers in a more or less direct manner to these same realities.[24]

It is true that Abhishiktananda many times referred to the tensions arising out of the simultaneous "presence of the *Upanishads* and the Gospel in a single heart" and that he occasionally used the language of fulfillment when addressing Christians, but this would seem to have been a case of *upaya*, "skilful means" as the Buddhists have it, "saving mirages." As Schuon observes, "In religious esoterisms, efficacy at times takes the place of truth, and rightly so, given the nature of the men to whom they are addressed."[25] In Abhishiktananda's case we can trace through his writings a move *away* from all notions of Christian exclusivism and triumphalism, *towards* the *sophia perennis*. All the evidence suggests that Abhishiktananda did indeed undergo the plenary experience and see that Light that, in Koranic terms, is "neither of the East nor of the West." In communicating that experience, and the knowledge that it delivers, Abhishiktananda felt comfortable resorting to the spiritual vocabulary of both theistic Christianity and monistic Vedanta. Take, for instance, passages such as these:

> The knowledge (vidya) of Christ is identical with what the Upanishads call divine knowledge (brahmavidya).... It comprises the whole of God's self-manifestation in time, and is one with his eternal self-manifestation.[26]

> Step by step I descended into what seemed to me to be successive depths of my true self—my being (sat), my awareness of being (cit), and my joy in being (ananda). Finally nothing was left but he himself, the Only One, infinitely alone, Being, Awareness and Bliss, Saccidananda.[27]

In his Introduction to the English edition of *Saccidananda*, Abhishiktananda states:

> Dialogue may begin simply with relations of mutual sympathy. It only becomes worthwhile when it is accompanied by full openness ... not merely at the intellectual level, but with regard to [the] inner life of the Spirit. Dialogue about doctrines will be more fruitful when it is rooted in a real spiritual experience at depth and when each one understands that diversity does not mean disunity, once the Centre of all has been reached.[28]

One measure of Abhishiktananda's mystical extinction in Advaitic non-dualism, and the problems this posed for some of his Christian contemporaries (and for all rigidly theistic theologies), is evident in a talk he prepared in the last months of his life:

> In this annihilating experience [of *Advaita*, non-dualism] one is no longer able to project in front of oneself anything whatsoever, to recognize any other "pole" to which to refer oneself and to give the name of God. Once one has reached that innermost center, one is so forcibly seized by the mystery that one can no longer utter a "Thou" or an "I." Engulfed in the abyss, we disappear to our own eyes, to our own consciousness. The proximity of that mystery which the prophetic traditions name "God" burns us so completely that there is no longer any question of discovering it in the depths of oneself or oneself in the depths of it. In the very engulfing, the gulf has vanished. If a cry was still possible—at the moment perhaps of disappearing into the abyss—it would be paradoxically: "but there is no abyss, no gulf, no distance!" There is no face-to-face, for there is only That-Which-Is, and no other to name it.[29]

This passage, reminiscent of Eckhart, can take its place among the most exalted of mystical commentaries; it also dispels any doubts as to the validity and fullness of Abhishiktananda's own mystical annihilation, called by whatever name.

The last decade of Abhishiktananda's life saw the publication of a series of books bearing the fragrance of his long years of prayer, meditation, study, and spiritual awakening. The English-language versions of these books are: *The Mountain of the Lord* (1966), an account of his pilgrimage to Gangotri, the sacred source of the Ganges; *Prayer* (1967); *Hindu-Christian Meeting Point* (1969); *The*

Church in India (1969); *Towards the Renewal of the Indian Church* (1970); *Saccidananda: A Christian Experience of Advaita* (1974), probably his most mature theological work; *Guru and Disciple* (1974); *The Secret of Arunachala* (1974), in which he recalls his experiences with Ramana and with Gnanananda; and *The Further Shore* (1975), his deepest meditation on the *Upanishads* and the ideal of *sannyasa*. A collection of several of his essays appeared posthumously as *The Eyes of Light* (1979).

There can be no doubt that, in the words of his friend Raimundo Panikkar, Abhishiktananda was "one of the most authentic witnesses of our times of the encounter in depth between Christian and Eastern spiritualities."[30] But his significance goes well beyond this. In his last work, *The Further Shore*, Abhishiktananda writes movingly and wisely of the ideal of the *sannyasi*:

> *Sannyasa* confronts us with a sign of that which is essentially beyond all signs—indeed, in its sheer transparency [to the Absolute] it proclaims its own death as a sign.... However the *sannyasi* lives in the world of signs, of the divine manifestation, and this world of manifestation needs him, "the one beyond signs," so that it may realize the impossible possibility of a bridge between the two worlds.... The sign of *sannyasa* ... stands then on the very frontier, the unattainable frontier. Between two worlds, the world of manifestation and the world of the unmanifest Absolute. It is the mystery of the sacred lived with the greatest possible interiority. It is a powerful means of grace—that grace which is nothing else than the Presence of the Absolute, the Eternal, the Unborn, existing at the heart of the realm of becoming, of time, of death and life; and a grace which is at the same time the irresistible drawing of the entire universe and its fullness towards the ultimate fullness of the Awakening to the Absolute, to the *Atman*.... Finally, it is even the *taraka*, the actual one who himself carries men across to the other shore, the one and only "ferryman," manifested in manifold ways in the form of all those rishis, mahatmas, gurus, and buddhas, who throughout history have themselves been woken and in turn awaken their brother-men.[31]

Abhishiktananda himself came to embody and to live this ideal. No man could have a more sublime epitaph.

Thomas Merton

1915–1968

A Monk for Our Time

The monastery is neither a museum nor an asylum.
The monk remains in the world from which he has fled,
and he remains a potent, though hidden, force in that world…[1]

homas Merton must surely be the best-known Christian monk of the century. His autobiographical *The Seven Storey Mountain* (1948) covering his early life, his conversion to Catholicism, and his decision to become a monk, has been a perennial favorite and is regarded by many as one of the exemplary spiritual documents of our times.[2] For all its freshness, it is, on Merton's own admission, a somewhat gauche work and slightly marred by the sentimental excesses of a recent convert. Merton himself seems to have been addicted to writing, producing a massive corpus of books (historical, theological, autobiographical, devotional, exegetical), articles, reviews, letters, journals, stories, manuals, memoirs, poetry, meditations—an almost exhaustive repertoire of literary genres. In turn he has generated an unflagging Merton industry, excavating his life and work in stupefying detail. On offer here is a skeletal account of his life and then some remarks about his central concerns.

Merton was born in France in 1915, his mother a cultured and sensitive woman from a well-to-do American family, his father an artist from New Zealand.[3] Thomas's mother died when he was six, his father when he was fifteen. The boy lived a somewhat peripatetic existence in the USA, England, and France, attending boarding schools on either side of the English Channel. Religion was a somewhat marginal affair in family life, though his father, Owen, was a nature mystic of sorts while the principal characteristic of the somewhat anodyne Christianity of his American relatives seems to have been a mild anti-Catholicism. Merton early revealed a gift for writing, producing two novels by the age of twelve, contributing poetry, stories, and reviews to school magazines. He was weak in mathematics and took an early dislike to Plato and Socrates, matched by an enthusiasm for Blake, on whom he wrote a postgraduate thesis at Columbia University. His first significant spiritual experience was at the age of about sixteen when he was

> overwhelmed with a sudden and profound insight into the misery and corruption of my own soul . . . and my soul desired escape and liberation and freedom from all this with an intensity and an urgency unlike anything I had ever known before . . . for the first time in my life I really began to pray. . . .[4]

Merton studied at Cambridge, and before leaving England had a brief affair which resulted in the birth of a child; it troubled his conscience for many years thereafter. (Both mother and child were killed in a bombing raid during the war.) As a student at Columbia Merton hurled himself into a bohemian lifestyle, becoming a habitué of coffee shops, wine bars, and jazz cellars in Greenwich Village as well as taking an active part in university literary circles and student politics. His political interests were sharpened by a visit to Cuba, where he felt a close identification with the poor.

While at Columbia Merton met a Hindu *sannyasi* who urged him to read St Augustine's *Confessions*. Other way-stations on the path to the monastery included Etienne Gilson's *The Spirit of Medieval Philosophy* and Huxley's *The Perennial Philosophy*, the works of Jacques Maritain, the poetry of Blake and Hopkins, and a visit to France, where he was ravished by the beauty of the medieval churches. In 1938 he was baptized, and within two years had decided to enter the priesthood:

> Now I had entered into the everlasting movement of that gravitation which is the very life and spirit of God: God's own gravitation towards the depth of His own infinite nature, His goodness without end. And God, that center Who is everywhere, and whose circumference is nowhere, finding me.... And He called out to me from His own immense depths.[5]

On an Easter retreat in 1941 he thrilled with the discovery of the world of the Trappists, Carthusians, and Camaldolese. He had discovered the Catholic expression of the ancient ideal of renunciation:

> What wonderful happiness there was, then, in the world! There were still men on this miserable, noisy, cruel earth, who tasted the marvelous joy of silence and solitude, who dwelt in forgotten mountain cells, in secluded monasteries.... They were poor, they had nothing, and therefore they were free and possessed everything, and everything they touched struck off something of the fire of divinity....[6]

The road to the monastery gates turned out to be full of hazards, but finally, in 1948, Merton was accepted as a novice at Gethsemani, a Trappist monastery in Kentucky.

The story of Merton's twenty years in the monastery has been told, in intricate detail, in Michael Mott's door-stopper, *The Seven Mountains of Thomas Merton*, the most complete biography we have. Some of the recurring motifs: Merton's love of the ancient rhythms of both the natural and the liturgical seasons; his devotion to the monastic ideal; his urgent advocacy of ecclesiastical and monastic reform coupled to his commitment to ecumenical and interreligious dialogue; his often prickly relationship with his superiors (complicated by Merton's rapidly growing celebrity as an author); his extraordinary fecundity as a writer and his torrential correspondence with artists, intellectuals, musicians, activists, spiritual leaders; his yearning for a more radical solitude married to his passionate engagement with the political and social issues of the day (race relations, Latin American politics, the Cold War, the nuclear threat, the brutalities of totalitarian regimes, Vietnam, the pervasive violence of modern life, the environmental crisis). Despite his enclaustration, Merton maintained warm relationships with many intellectuals and spiritual leaders—Mark van Doren, Thich Nat Hanh (who wrote a poem entitled "Thomas Merton is My Brother"), Daniel Berrigan, Rosemary Radford Ruether, Czeslaw Milosz, Marco Pallis, D. T. Suzuki, to name but a few.

By the early '60s Merton had immersed himself not only in the "waters of silence" but in the mystical literature of Taoism, Tibetan and Zen Buddhism, Hinduism, and Sufism. In the decade before his death he produced a series of strikingly fresh, often poetic, and profound works. In 1968, after years of conflict with his abbot, Merton was finally allowed to go on a long-desired trip to Asia, principally to participate in an interreligious monastic conference in Bangkok, but also to make a pilgrimage to the sacred sites of India and South-East Asia and to meet representatives of the Eastern traditions. Merton's sojourn in Asia was abruptly ended when, apparently, he was fatally electrocuted by a faulty appliance in his hotel room in Bangkok.[7]

Merton's writings have been a delight to readers all over the world. The early works are confined within the sometimes claustrophobic walls of mid-century Catholic piety, but Merton's understanding of the spiritual life, of the centrality of mystical experience, and of the inter-relations of the great religious patrimonies of both

East and West gradually matured into one of the most profound spiritual visions of the century. Both in his person and in his work he came to be a conduit for some of the deepest spiritual currents of our times. Before turning to Merton's encounter with the East, mention must be made of a few of his more singular and enduring works on Christian and Western themes: *The Waters of Siloe* (1949), a monastic history; *The Silent Life* (1957), a limpid account of the monastic ideal; *New Seeds of Contemplation* (1961), the most beautiful of Merton's meditations on Christian spirituality; *Conjectures of a Guilty Bystander* (1966), an arresting collection of fragments on contemporary political issues; *Raids on the Unspeakable* (1966), which includes some of Merton's most lively and imaginative literary work. His literary essays, poems, letters, and journals (in six volumes) have been posthumously published, as well as countless anthologies. When T. S. Eliot was asked his view of Merton's poetry he sternly replied that he wrote too much and should be more careful.[8] Marco Pallis makes the same reproach about Merton's output as a whole[9]—and coming from a writer who himself took the most scrupulous care to treat the religious subjects about which he wrote with both the precision and the formality that he thought their due, one is not entirely unsympathetic to the observation. But perhaps this is to misunderstand the nature of Merton's peculiar gifts as a writer: his deficiencies are, in a sense, the very token of his virtues as a writer: immediacy, spontaneity, fluidity, the sense of a real presence, often humorous, sometimes acerbic, very rarely dull.

Throughout his last journey, Merton kept a haphazard collection of notes and jottings that were compiled after his death and published as *The Asian Journal of Thomas Merton*. The book gives a very immediate and intimate sense of Merton's exhilaration as he meets his fellow-monks in India, Ceylon, and Thailand, visits sacred sites, returns to the ancient scriptures, ponders the art and architecture of India, meets with spiritual leaders. He also refers to the reading matter in his kit-bag for his various journeyings: Sankara, Milarepa, Ramanuja, Masao Abe, Aelred Graham, Evans-Wentz, Tucci, Hermann Hesse, Abhishiktananda, Dasgupta, T. R. V. Murti, Marco Pallis, Edward Conze, and many more—a veritable East-West library! Despite its fragmentary nature *The Asian Journal* is at once charming, piercingly insightful, often moving. All of it testifies to Merton's extraordinary receptivity to the spiritual messages emanating from the people, the temples, shrines and stupas, the artworks, the landscape itself. Here, for instance, is the passage describing his experience before the Buddha figures of Polonnaruwa, somewhat reminiscent of Rudolf Otto's encounter with the *mysterium tremendum* in the statues of Elephanta:

> The path dips down to Gal Vihara: a wide, quiet, hollow, surrounded by trees. A low outcrop of rock, with a cave cut into it, and beside the cave a big seated Buddha on the left, a reclining Buddha on the right, and Ananda, I guess, standing by the head of the reclining Buddha. In the cave, another seated Buddha. The vicar general [Merton's host], shying away from "paganism," hangs back and sits under a tree reading the guidebook. I am able to approach the Buddha barefoot and undisturbed, my feet in wet grass, wet sand. Then the silence of the extraordinary faces. The great smiles. Huge and yet subtle. Filled with every possibility, questioning nothing, knowing everything, rejecting nothing, the peace not of emotional resignation but of *Madhyamika*, of *sunyata*, that has seen through every question without trying to discredit anyone or anything—without refutation—without establishing some other argument. For the doctrinaire, the mind that needs well-established positions, such peace, such silence, can be frightening. I was knocked over with a rush of relief and thankfulness at the obvious clarity of the figures, the clarity and fluidity of shape and line, the design of the monumental bodies composed into the rock shape and landscape, figure, rock and tree.... Looking at these figures I was suddenly, almost forcibly, jerked clean out of the habitual, half-tied vision of things, and an inner clearness, clarity, as if exploding from the rocks themselves, became evident and obvious. The queer evidence of the reclining figure, the smile, the sad smile of Ananda standing with his arms folded (much more "imperative" than Da Vinci's *Mona Lisa* because completely simple and straightforward). The thing about all this is that there is no puzzle, no problem, and really no "mystery." All problems are resolved and everything is clear, simply because what matters is clear. The rock, all matter, all life, is charged with *Dharmakaya* ... everything is emptiness and everything is compassion. I don't know when in my

life I have ever had such a sense of beauty and spiritual validity running together in one aesthetic illumination. Surely, with Mahabalipuram and Polonnaruwa my Asian pilgrimage has come clear and purified itself. I mean, I know and have seen what I was obscurely looking for. I don't know what else remains but I have now seen and have pierced through the surface and have got beyond the shadow and the disguise. This is Asia in its purity, not covered over with garbage, Asian or European or American, and it is clear, pure, complete. It says everything; it needs nothing. And because it is needs nothing it can afford to be silent, unnoticed, undiscovered. It does not need to be discovered. It is we, Asians included, who need to discover it.[10]

On this trip Merton had three cordial meetings with the Dalai Lama who, when he was later asked whether he believed in God replied, "It depends what you mean by 'God': if you mean by 'God' what Thomas Merton means, then yes, I do." Merton also had fruitful encounters with many other monks of the Tibetan diaspora including Chögyam Trungpa, Kalu Rinpoche, and Chatral Rinpoche, with Theravadins such as Nyanaponika Thera, the English Bikkhu Phra Khantipalo, and with scholars and writers such as Lobsang Lhalungpa and Dr Raghavan.

Most of Merton's writings on the Eastern traditions can be found in his introductions to *The Way of Chuang Tzu* (1965) (the "translation" of which he described as the most enjoyable project of his life) and *Gandhi on Non-Violence* (1965), and two collections of essays on Eastern subjects, *Mystics and Zen Masters* (1967) and *Zen and the Birds of Appetite* (1968). Here we might recall that the redoubtable D.T. Suzuki believed Merton to be one of very few Westerners who fully understood Zen.[11] Certainly Merton's several essays on Zen match anything of comparable intent written by a Westerner.[12]

As intimated earlier, there is now a Merton publishing industry: the rivers of ink continue to flow freely. Here we may mention just a few works of interest. Of the several biographies of Merton the most exhaustive is Mott's aforementioned *The Seven Mountains of Thomas Merton* (1984), while two sympathetic but not uncritical biographies of more modest proportions are Monica Furlong's well-known *Merton: A Biography* (1980) and a book that deserves a much wider audience, William Shannon's *Silent Lamp: The Thomas Merton Story* (1992), in many respects the most penetrating of the three. A collection of photos and reminiscences by his friend John Howard Griffin, *A Hidden Wholeness*, presents an intimate portrait of Merton and his life at Gethsemani. (Griffin was a writer, photographer, and author of the remarkable *Black Like Me*.) Among the more percipient commentators on Merton's work are William Shannon, Patrick Hart, Marco Pallis, Henri Nouwen, Thérèse Lentfoehr, Walter Capps, Bonnie Thurston, Peter Francis, and George Woodcock.

In the present context it is quite impossible to do justice to Merton's immense contribution to the intellectual and spiritual life of our times. Nor can we here measure his impact on the development of more open and creative communication between the religions of Occident and Orient. However, we can take note of some of the persistent Mertonian themes that mark his writings on interreligious subjects: the indispensability to spiritual vitality of contemplation, meditation, prayer; the inadequacy of language to express spiritual experience, and the dangers of the Western preoccupation with definition, measurement, conceptualization, and analysis; the role of solitude in nurturing an understanding of the illusory nature of the egoic self; the universality of the monastic ideal (even where it is not institutionalized, as in Islam); the rejection of the rationalist-masculinist-instrumentalist paradigm of Western modernity; the notion that creative dialogue springs from a commitment to and knowledge of one's own tradition, and from an open heart; the West's need for much more *wu wei*—the "creative quietitude" of Chuang Tzu and the Taoist masters; the reconciliation of the opposites; the relevance to the West of the Gandhian ideals of *ahimsa* (non-injuriousness), *satyagraha* ("truth-force"), and *brahmacharya* (self-control, renunciation), all informed by the *Gita's* teaching of non-attachment to the fruits of one's action; the spiritual potentialities of expressive modes such as painting, music, and poetry; the critique of the anti-mystical, exclusivist, and legalistic posture of some ecclesiastical institutions and authorities; the liberating power of love and compassion; the impermanence and "emptiness" of all phenomena.

By way of a conclusion we shall make do with a sample of fragments from Merton's writings, each suggestive of the themes and
preoccupations which concerned him most deeply.

A Miscellany of Fragments from Father Louis (Thomas Merton)

Let us face the fact that the monastic vocation tends to present
itself to the modern world as a problem and as a scandal. In a basi-
cally religious culture, like that of India, or of Japan, the monk is
more or less taken for granted (*The Silent Life*).

The monk acts on the world simply by being a monk ... in the
loneliness of his detachment he has a far higher vocation to char-
ity than anyone else... (*The Silent Life*).

The vocation to solitude is ... to become fully awake (*The Power
and Meaning of Love*).

Contemplation is the highest expression of man's intellectual and
spiritual life. It is that life itself, fully awake, fully active, fully
aware... (*New Seeds of Contemplation*).

God cannot be understood except by Himself (*New Seeds of Contemplation*).

One of the most widespread errors of our time is a superficial
"personalism" which identifies the "person" with the external self,
the empirical ego, and devotes itself solemnly to the cultivation of
this ego. But this is a cult of pure illusion, the illusion of what is
popularly imagined to be "personality" or worse still "dynamic"
and "successful" personality. When this error is taken over into
religion it leads to the worst kind of nonsense, a cult of psycholo-
gism and self-expression which vitiates our whole cultural and
spiritual self (*New Seeds of Contemplation*).

That which is oldest is most young and most new. There is nothing so ancient and so dead as human novelty. The "latest" is always
stillborn. What is really new is what was there all the time (*New
Seeds of Contemplation*).

I believe that by openness to Buddhism, to Hinduism, and to these
great Asian traditions, we stand a wonderful chance of learning
more about the potentiality of our own traditions... (*Asian Journal*).

The monk is a man who, in one way or another, pushes to the frontiers of human experience and strives to go beyond, to find out what transcends the ordinary level of existence ("Renewal and Discipline").

It was the spiritual consciousness of a people that was awakened in the spirit of one person [Gandhi]. But the message of the Indian spirit, of Indian wisdom, was not for India alone. It was for the entire world (*Gandhi on Non-Violence*).

Such men (true solitaries), out of pity for the universe, out of loyalty to mankind, and without a spirit of bitterness or resentment, withdraw into the healing silence of the wilderness, or of poverty, or of obscurity, not in order to preach to others but to heal in themselves the wounds of the whole world.[13]

It is absolutely essential to introduce into our study of the humanities a dimension of wisdom oriented to contemplation as well as wise action. For this, it is no longer sufficient merely to go back over the Christian and European cultural tradition. The horizons of the world are no longer confined to Europe and America. We have to gain new spiritual perspectives, and on this our spiritual, and even our physical survival may depend (*Mystics and Zen Masters*).

Huston Smith

1919–2016

Bridge-Builder

The larger the island of knowledge,
the longer the shoreline of wonder.[1]

f Rudolf Otto's *The Idea of the Holy* and William James's *The Varieties of Religious Experience* were two of the most widely read books on religion of the inter-war period, Huston Smith's *The Religions of Man* must surely be the most popular of the second half of the twentieth century. First published in 1958, it has been in print ever since, selling millions of copies and now retitled *The World's Religions: Our Great Wisdom Traditions*. The hallmarks of Smith's approach to the comparative study of the world's religions were evident from the outset: the conviction that each religion was the custodian of timeless truths and values; the attempt to understand the forms and practices of any particular tradition from the viewpoint of its adherents; an intuitive sympathy that enabled Smith to "tune into" a wide diversity of spiritual modalities; an understanding that the hyper-rationalism of much modern philosophy and the pseudo-scientific methodologies of the so-called social sciences were inadequate tools with which to grasp spiritual realities; a style of exposition free of the specialized jargon of the disciplines on which Smith drew (most notably philosophy, theology, comparative religion) and one immediately accessible to the intelligent general reader. One might say that Smith's mode turned on a kind of natural courtesy and respect for the traditions he was exploring. He also situated the study of religion within an existential context:

> Religion alive confronts the individual with the most momentous option this world can present. It calls the soul to the highest adventure it can undertake, a proposed journey across the jungles, peaks, and deserts of the human spirit. The call is to confront reality, to master the self. Those who dare to hear and follow this secret call soon learn the dangers and difficulties of its lonely journey.[2]

Clearly, for Smith the study of religion was no mere academic exercise but one of deep engagement. He would likely agree with the claim of another inter-religious bridge-builder, Fr Bede Griffiths, that, "The rediscovery of religion is the great intellectual, moral, and spiritual adventure of our time."[3]

Since 1958 Smith's understanding of both the inner unity and the formal diversity of the world's integral religious traditions was both deepened and sharpened by his encounter with the traditionalist perspective exemplified in the works of such figures as René Guénon, Ananda Coomaraswamy, and Frithjof Schuon. As was clear from the 1991 revisions to *The Religions of Man*, Smith's horizons had also broadened to encompass the primordial traditions of peoples such as the Native Americans.[4] Within the academic world Smith was a passionate and eloquent spokesman for the perennialist school, and engaged many of the deepest problems and issues arising out of the contemporary collision of the forces of tradition and modernity. His essential vocation was as an *educator* and, to use his own term, a *"religious communicator."* Recently Smith recalled the impact made on him as a fourteen-year old by Kipling's poem, "The Explorer," which includes these lines:

> Something hidden, go and find it;
> Go and look behind the ranges.
> Something lost behind the ranges;
> Lost and waiting for you—go!

He writes that the poem still haunted him in his old age. *Exploration*—both intellectual and spiritual—might also be seen as a keynote of Smith's long adventure in the mystery of life.

Smith was born in 1919 in Soochow, China.[5] His parents were missionaries and he was to spend the first seventeen years of his life in China, lovingly recounted in his autobiography, *Tales of Wonder* (2009). One of his former students, Philip Novak, writes:

> If you would know Huston Smith, start with China.... Beholding him, one wonders whether fantastic tales about Chinese magic are not true after all. There is something distantly—and yet distinctly—Asian in his physiognomy. China paused on his skin, it seemed, before proceeding to his marrow.... Open the pages of the *Analects* to Confucius's description of the *chun-tzu* (ideal gentleman) and you touch Huston's fiber. *Chun-tzu* ... one who possesses a truly human heart, who cherishes the arts of learning and teaching, and who is as concerned to teach by moral example as by intellectual knack.[6]

After his schooling at the Shanghai American School, Smith studied at the Central Methodist College in Fayette, Missouri, where his intellectual engagements were primarily theological and philosophical. Thereafter he pursued further studies at the prestigious Divinity School at the University of Chicago and at the University of California Berkeley, during which time, partly under the influence of the "Californian Vedantins" (Gerald Heard and Aldous Huxley among them) he became more deeply engaged in the study of mysticism. A series of teaching appointments followed at the universities of Denver and Colorado, Washington University in St Louis, the Massachusetts Institute of Technology (1958–1973) and Syracuse University (1973–1983). Early in his career Smith also served as a chaplain and associate minister in the Methodist Church, improbably combining these duties with the presidency of the St Louis Vedanta Society! In later years Smith became one of the prime movers in the establishment of the Foundation of Traditional Studies, based in Washington DC, of which he was vice-president. As the editor of a *Festschrift* in his honor remarked,

> Professor Smith's teaching career has been devoted to bridging intellectual gulfs: between East and West, between science and the humanities, and between the formal education of the classroom and informal education via films and television.[7]

His films and television programs focused on Hinduism, Buddhism, Sufism, and Tibetan music. In 1996 Bill Moyers hosted a five-part PBS television series, *The Wisdom of Faith with Huston Smith*. I like Smith's recollection about science and religion: "Science makes major contributions to minor needs, Justice Holmes was fond of saying, adding that religion, however small its successes, is at least at work on the things that matter most."[8]

From Smith's wide-ranging scholarly *oeuvre*, which came to include fourteen books, we may select three works of signal importance: *The Religions of Man*, a masterly and engaging conspectus of the world's major religious traditions; *Forgotten Truth: the Primordial Tradition* (1977), in which he expounds the perennial wisdom that lies at the heart of manifold sapiential doctrines and religious forms; and *Beyond the Post-Modern Mind* (1982), which elaborates a critique of the intellectual habits and prejudices of the prevailing contemporary worldview, particularly as it finds expression in the Western Academy (which no longer really deserves the name) and in the highly reductive disciplinary specializations that purport to "explain" religious phenomena. As well as these three major landmarks we should note a recent anthology of some of Smith's most important articles, *Essays on World Religion* (1992), which includes many pieces on Asian subjects. A sample of titles indicates the range of Smith's interests: "Transcendence in Traditional China," "Tao Now: An Ecological Statement," "A Note on Shinto," "Spiritual Discipline in Zen," "India and the Infinite," "Vedic Religion and the Soma Experience," "The Importance of the Buddha," "Tibetan Chant: Inducing the Spirit." Smith's understanding of his own tradition is most fully explained in *The Soul of Christianity: Restoring the Great Tradition* (2005), of which Pico Iyer wrote:

> Smith has long been our clearest and most radiant explorer of all the world's great religions. But in this book he writes with a new urgency and brilliance, to shake us from our stupor and remind us of a beautiful tradition too often lost or mistreated. Thank heavens for such wisdom, delivered with light and fire.[9]

In his Preface Smith observed that the writing of this particular book was exhilarating because it enabled him to discern more clearly "the intellectual and spiritual gold of Christianity, its intellectual expanse, the vastness of its atmosphere, and its genius for cutting through to the quick of life."[10] I think we may suppose that Smith's lifelong exploration of other spiritual universes brought him to a richer understanding of his own religious heritage. Not an uncommon story.

The most decisive shift in Smith's outlook occurred as a consequence of reading the works of Frithjof Schuon, the master expositor of the *religio perennis* in modern times. Smith had been introduced to the works of Guénon, Schuon, and other traditionalists by Seyyed Hossein Nasr during his time at MIT. Smith:

> I discovered that [Schuon] situated the world's religious traditions in a framework that enabled me to honor their significant differences unreservedly while at the same time seeing them as expressions of a truth, that because it was single, I could affirm. In a

single stroke I was handed a way of honoring the world's diversity without falling prey to relativism, a resolution I had been seeking for more than thirty years.[11]

The influence of perennialism also made itself felt in Smith's ever-deepening interest in mysticism as the esoteric kernel within the exoteric shell of all integral traditions. This perspective not only placed Smith's understanding of mystical traditions—especially Sufism—on a much firmer footing, but also allowed him to honor fully the orthodox religious forms which veil and protect that ultimately formless wisdom which lies at the heart of the *sophia peren-nis*.

One of the penalties of fame is the exposure to endless invitations to write Prefaces, Forewords, Introductions, and the like. It is a measure of both Smith's international standing and his generosity of spirit to note some of the books he helped introduce to a wider audience, many of which have become classics of their kind: *The Three Pillars of Zen* (1967) by Philip Kapleau, *A Buddhist Bible* (1970) by Dwight Godard, *Zen Mind, Beginner's Mind* (1970) by Shunryu Suzuki, *Ideals and Realities of Islam* (1972) by S.H. Nasr, *The Transcendent Unity of Religions* (1975) by Frithjof Schuon, *The Spiritual Heritage of India* (1979) by Swami Prabhavananda, *On Having No Head* (1986) by D.E. Harding, *A Treasury of Traditional Wisdom* (1986) edited by Whitall Perry, *Mysticism and Philosophy* (1987) by W.T. Stace, *The Wheel of Life* (1988) by John Blofeld, and a new edition of *The Way of a Pilgrim and the Pilgrim Continues His Way* (1991). I was humbled by Smith's gracious Foreword to my own *Journeys East* (2004).

While the Judeo-Christian tradition in which he was raised provided Smith with a firm spiritual anchorage, his life and work alike testify to his willingness to immerse himself in the religious forms and practices of other traditions, not by way of any kind of syncretism or "universal" religion, but in the search for understanding and for "the light that is of neither East nor West."[12] Religious *experience* was a watchword in his writings, and among his own spiritual encounters we may note his boyhood exposure to a Confucian master, his spell as a Methodist minister, weekly sessions with a Vedantin swami, the practice of yoga, and an intensive reading of the

Upanishads and other Hindu Scriptures in the 1950s, a summer of meditation and *koan*-training in a Myoshinji monastery in Kyoto in the '60s (where he studied under Master Goto Zuigan, developed a close friendship with D.T. Suzuki, doyen of modern Zen scholars, and practiced *zazen* with Gary Snyder), his inquiries into the possible links between drug-induced experiences and mysticism, his close association with traditionalist Sufis in Iran and the USA. He was a sympathetic and no doubt exemplary guest in many Houses of the Spirit. As well as moving freely through the corridors of academia (where, it must be said, his ideas encountered some suspicion and scepticism as well as acclaim) he met countless rabbis, clerics, swamis, Zen masters, lamas, mystics and the like; by all reports such meetings were marked by that rapport which arises out of the spontaneous and mutual recognition of the radiant spiritual maturity which marks those who have traveled a goodly distance on the path.

As an educator and communicator Huston Smith always displayed a gift for articulating profound truths in the most simple and accessible language. Here is an example from his recent autobiography, one which also intimates the mystery which, he tells us, can hardly be fathomed in a lifetime.[13] Referring to the cross as "the metaphor I use for understanding human existence," Smith writes:

> Our life in historical or chronological time, measuring and minding, cautious and comparing, forms the horizontal arm of the cross. Our experience of the unqualified, of inner, immeasurable time (or timelessness), is the cross's vertical pole. We live in two kinds of time or perspective simultaneously. The horizontal and the vertical are at once quite distinct and entirely overlapping, and to experience their incongruity and confluence is what it means to be human.[14]

In the conclusion to the most recent edition of *The World's Religions* the author observed that we have just survived "the bloodiest of centuries; but if its ordeals are to be birth pangs rather than death throes, the century's scientific advances must be matched by comparable advances in human relations." Such advances depend on our ability to *listen* to voices from all over the planet and to nurture a peace built not on ecclesiastical or political hegemonies but on under-standing and mutual concern. For understanding, at least in realms as inherently noble as the great faiths of mankind, brings respect; and respect prepares the way for a higher power, love—the only power that can quench the flames of fear, suspicion, and prejudice, and provide the means by which the people of this small but precious Earth can become one to one another.[15]

Huston Smith: scholar, minister, teacher, culture critic, pilgrim, bridge-builder; in each of these roles he has served the cause of interreligious understanding with great distinction and, in the words of one of his students, with "honesty of person, penetrating sensitivity . . . and flowing kindness."[16]

Philip Sherrard

1922–1995

Orthodox Perennialist

*We are faced with a challenge, an issue of life or
death: either to affirm the eternal nature of our being . . .
or to acquiesce in our own dehumanization and eclipse in obedience
to the forces that with our cooperation have fabricated the infernal
and artificial forms of the contemporary world.*[1]

t the tail-end of World War I, Philip Sherrard was sent to Greece as a British soldier. His life was forever changed by this encounter. He seems to have been more or less spontaneously transformed into a fervent Graecophile. He had been born in Oxford, into a family with connections to the Bloomsbury crowd in which the prevailing outlook was that of a "liberal scientific humanism" that Sherrard was soon to disown. He studied history at Cambridge and developed an early interest in German Romanticism. Returning home after his military duty in Athens, accompanied by his new Greek wife (with whom he had two daughters), Sherrard embarked on doctoral studies in modern Greek poetry at London University and established friendly relations with several Greek writers, George Seferis among them.[2] His doctoral thesis was eventually published as *The Marble Threshing Floor: Studies in Modern Greek Poetry* (1956). He returned to Greece to take up the position of Assistant Director of the British Archaeological School in Athens. His deepening interest in the Orthodox tradition prompted the first of several visits to Mt Athos, where he was to come under the influence of a Russian hermit, Fr Nikon of Karoulia, who instructed him in the practice of the Jesus Prayer. He was formally baptized in 1956. One of the attractions of Orthodoxy was what Sherrard saw as its preservation of an organic connection between humankind and the rest of the natural order, a theme he would foreground in his later writings.

In the next two decades Sherrard moved between England and Greece, and held various research and teaching posts at the Royal Institute of International Affairs, St Anthony's College, Oxford, King's College, Cambridge, and the School of Slavonic and East European Studies. In 1977 he moved permanently to Greece with his second wife, the publisher Denise Harvey, living a simple existence in a rustic cottage (no electricity, no phone) on the northern island of Evia. He was a connoisseur of the locally-grown wines and wrote a rhapsodic piece "In Praise of Wine," later published in the *Temenos Journal*.[3]

No occasion, whether civic banquet or private gathering graced by the intimacies of good talk and the warmth of friendship, is complete without wine. Not swilled, but sipped, deliberately, slowly, lovingly, every drop savored, its smell tantalizing the nostrils, its color the eyes, gradually, as glass succeeds glass, it produces the inner transformation that allows thought to flow more freely, the heart to burgeon, the tones and harmonies of life to grow more rich and beautiful. Those who have mastered the art of drinking wine know that they belong to an exalted company, share secrets of which others are ignorant, have entered a world of mystery where they are released from the frustrations and fears, the drabness and triviality that so bedevil ordinary human existence.

Sherrard died in 1995. The funeral rites were conducted in a simple stone chapel which he and his wife had built near their home, looking across to Mt Parnassus on the mainland.[4]

Sherrard's god-daughter, Julie du Boulay, recounts an episode in which we glimpse something of Sherrard's make-up. During his wartime service in Italy he was accepting the surrender of a German officer who refused to relinquish his weapon, asking Sherrard what he would do in the same circumstances. Sherrard removed his revolver from its holster and put it on a table between them. The gun was made of wood! Sherrard did not wish to carry a real one. Du Boulay observes, "This story reveals some of Philip's most endearing characteristics—a willingness to risk himself, a love of peace, an utter lack of pomposity, an ability to be just slightly out of step with more conventional thinking."[5]

Sherrard deserves our attention on several counts: as a scholar, translator, and expositor of Greek letters, more generally of Hellenic history, and, most significantly, of the Orthodox tradition that suffused the whole culture; as one of the founders of the Temenos Academy; as a perennialist philosopher; and lastly as one of the most percipient commentators on what he called "the rape of nature," the title of one of his most important books (his Western publishers sanitized the title to *The Eclipse of Nature*.[6])

Sherrard produced a range of writings—translation, biography, critical commentary, memoir—on modern Greek literature, little known in the mid-century Anglosphere. Among the poets to whom he devoted the most sustained attention were George Seferis, Angelos Sikelianos, C.P. Cavafy, Costis Palamas, Nikos Kazantzakis, and

Odysseus Elytis. He was himself a poet and published several volumes of verse. Much of his translation and editorial work was done in collaboration with the American scholar Edmund Keeley. Sherrard's interests were religious and metaphysical as well as literary and aesthetic. As his wife wrote in an obituary,

> Philip Sherrard believed post-Byzantine life and culture in Greece to be essentially and organically related to the spiritual tradition of the Eastern Orthodox Church, and he dedicated his life to conveying something of both the culture and this spiritual tradition to the English-speaking world. His work was pioneering, and to many people he will have been the first to have introduced them to Orthodoxy as well as to modern Greek poetry. His work on Athos, Constantinople, and the breach in Christendom, have opened up new perspectives as much as his work on poetry, myth, and the imagination.[7]

The works in question include *Athos: Mountain of Silence, Constantinople: the Iconography of a Sacred City*; *The Greek East and the Latin West*; and *Church, Papacy, Schism: A Theological Enquiry*.

Sherrard's love of Greece is illuminated by a passage from the opening chapter of *The Wound of Greece: Studies in Neo-Hellenism* (1978), where he writes of

> the living fate of Greece, which is not a doom but a destiny, a process rather in which past and present blend and fuse, in which nature and man and something more than man participate: a process, difficult, baffling, enigmatic, with its element of magic, its element of tragedy, working itself out in a landscape of bare hills and insatiable sea, in the miraculous cruelty of the summer sun, in the long generations of the lives of Greek people.[8]

This passage reminds me of the intense and often visionary writings of Nikos Kazantzakis, of his blazing love of the land, the history, the people and the religious traditions of Greece.[9] It was a love shared by my late friend and colleague Roger Sworder.

Sherrard's most extended project was carried out in collaboration with Metropolitan Kallistos Ware and Gerald Palmer: the translation of *The Philokalia*, a corpus of religious texts and treatises dating back to the fourth century, a veritable treasure-house of Orthodox spirituality. It was only shortly before his death that Sherrard completed work on the fifth and final volume. Not only did Sherrard make the spiritual riches of the Orthodox tradition more widely known in the West but he had a significant impact on contemporary thought within the Church. Indeed, one commentator has suggested that Sherrard had as great an impact on modern Orthodox thought as any layman excepting only Vladimir Lossky.[10] Kallistos Ware, perhaps the most influential advocate of Orthodox spirituality in the contemporary West, commended Sherrard as "a creative and sometimes prophetic interpreter of the living tradition of the orthodox Church."[11] Nonetheless, and not surprisingly, Sherrard's perennialist perspective sometimes brought him into conflict with more doctrinaire theologians.[12] Sherrard was always up for a joust on matters religious and metaphysical.

In November 1986 a group of artists, writers, and scholars gathered in South Devon for the First Temenos Conference on the theme "Art and the Renewal of the Sacred." Among the attendees who were to play a crucial role in the subsequent establishment of the Temenos Academy were Kathleen Raine (poet, critic, philosopher), Keith Critchlow (architect and geometer), Brian Keeble (publisher and author), and Philip Sherrard. These four subsequently became the editors of the *Temenos Academy Review*, a successor to the *Temenos Journal* in which they had all been involved since its appearance in 1980. A blurb for the 1986 Conference announced its agenda:

> to reaffirm and redefine the function of the arts as the mirror of the human spirit. In the present situation society is suffering from the loss of any value-system which corresponds to our true needs and nature, and a new examination of the fundamental principles of life is of vital importance. From time immemorial the arts have been the medium for the expression and spreading of the human vision of the sacredness of life. At present the finer values in society have succumbed to the reductionist and materialist ideologies which threaten our very survival.[13]

Apart from those already mentioned, speakers at the conference included Wendell Berry, Jocelyn Godwin, Satish Kumar, and Yoshikazu Iwamoto. The Academy was formally established in 1991 under the patronage of the Prince of Wales. It presents courses in the perennial philosophy, which "runs like a golden thread through history and offers each generation contact with the values that nourish all civilizations"[14] (except, it should be added, our own). The Academy also sponsors public lectures and exhibitions, maintains the Review, and has a close association with the Prince's School of Traditional Arts. The website welcomes readers with a verse from Kathleen Raine:

> Against the *nihil*
> One candle flame, one blade of grass
> One thought suffices
> To affirm all.

(We might note in passing that Sherrard later mounted quite a severe critique of Kathleen Raine's understanding of the psyche and what he saw as her over-valuation of the Imagination.[15] Raine does not seem to have been unduly upset by his criticisms. After his death she wrote a generous and eloquent tribute to Sherrard.[16]) In The Marble Threshing Floor Sherrard had articulated a vision of art that was no doubt largely shared by his colleagues:

> The artistic process neither begins nor ends with the individual.... Art begins with a supra-individual world that cannot be known by observation or discursive reasoning but only by contemplation. This is the world of spiritual realities, of archetypes and archetypal experience, and it is the task of the artist to embody this world in [their] work.[17]

The poets on whom he had focused in his first book reveal to us, he said, "the actual participation of the temporal in the eternal."

The third salient feature of Sherrard's contribution to modern Christian thought is his perennialist perspective. I have been unable to discover precisely how Sherrard first came to perennialism. Guénon seems to have been the decisive influence. Of the French metaphysician Sherrard wrote this:

> If during the last century or so there has been even some slight revival of awareness in the western world of what is meant by metaphysics and the metaphysical tradition, the credit for it must go above all to Guénon. At a time when the confusion into which western thought had fallen was such that it threatened to obliter-

ate the few remaining traces of genuine spiritual knowledge from the minds and hearts of his contemporaries, Guénon, virtually single-handed, took it upon himself to reaffirm the values and principles which, he recognized, constitute the only sound basis for the living of a human life with dignity and purpose and for the formation of a civilization worthy of the name.[18]

We may also suppose that Sherrard's friendship with the Anglo-Greek mountaineer, musician, and initiate of Tibet Buddhism, Marco Pallis, was another factor in his commitment to perennialism. The perennialist school encompasses persons from all of the major integral religious traditions, but its preeminent exponents have been Sufis, while two of the most important thinkers in the first wave of traditionalism, Ananda Coomaraswamy and Marco Pallis, cleaved through personal affiliation to the Hindu and Buddhist traditions. Christian representatives within the perennialist school have been comparatively few in number and somewhat on the fringe. One may mention such people as Rama Coomaraswamy, Alvin Moore Jr, and Jean Borella. In the English-speaking world Sherrard, along with Huston Smith, James Cutsinger, and Wolfgang Smith, has been one of the leading Christian perennialists. In this role he has married his deep knowledge of Orthodox spirituality with a metaphysical framework that derives primarily from Guénonian perennialism.[19] Over many years of study and spiritual practice Sherrard immersed himself in the mystical and metaphysical writings of the Christian tradition and in the work of such contemporaries as Titus Burckhardt, Ananda Coomaraswamy, Henri Corbin, Yeats, Gershom Scholem, and C.S. Lewis. His own work is densely textured with references to some of the traditional writers by whom he was most deeply affected: Irenaeus, Clement of Alexandria, Plotinus, Origen, Maximos the Confessor, Gregory Palamas, Eckhart, Ruysbroeck, Jacob Boehme. As Kallistos Ware has observed, "Philip was genuinely Orthodox, but his vision of Orthodox Christianity was generous and wide-ranging, not defensive or timidly parochial. All too many Orthodox Christians today understand their faith as negation rather than affirmation."[20] The fruit of this marriage of traditional Christianity and perennialism is to be found in such works as *Christianity: Lineaments of a Sacred Tradition*

(1998), a posthumous compilation of Sherrard's most important essays on Christian subjects, and *Human Image, World Image: The Death and Resurrection of Sacred Cosmology* (1992). One of his particular and abiding interests was in a Christian understanding of sexuality, which he elaborated in *Christianity and Eros: Essays on the Theme of Sexual Love* (1976).

As intimated earlier, Sherrard's perennialism, especially as it related to "the transcendent unity of religions," caused some dismay among Orthodox theologians and scholars. Here, for instance, is James L. Kelley, previously deeply impressed by Sherrard's earlier writings, but now upset by his later work:

> It was only much later that I heard rumors of Philip Sherrard's bizarre comments concerning other "traditional faiths." A second friend whispered to me that "Sherrard is a perennialist". . . . I came to the conclusion that Sherrard had indeed, to judge by his final theological testament, Christianity: Lineaments of a Sacred Tradition, succumbed to the heretical teaching that God has saved and continues to save men through non-Christian religions. I remained disconcerted as to how such a seemingly staunch Orthodox traditionalist became misguided concerning these questions so central to Christian life and belief.

Kelley goes on to say that *"Despite his perennialism* Sherrard was able to use his knowledge of Orthodox Patristic writers to arrive at insights into the errant religious and secular developments of the West."[21] For my own part, I would say that it was precisely Sherrard's perennialist understanding that allowed him to fathom the metaphysical profundity and spiritual efficacy of those Orthodox texts which Kelley is at such pains to defend against "heretical teaching." Other Christian perennialists have inevitably run up against the kind of constricted religious exclusivism championed by the likes of Kelley.

In the last decade of his life, as well as maintaining a heroic labor on *The Philokalia*, Sherrard focused most of his intellectual energy on an analysis of the state of the contemporary world and the search for a way out. In *The Rape of Man and Nature* and *Human Image, World Image* he developed two interrelated themes: the destructive hegemony of the modern scientific worldview, particularly as it applied to human self-understanding, and the desperate need for a sacred cosmology proportioned to the most urgent needs of the era. If it be asked what is the modern worldview, we might call into service Lord Northbourne's characterization of it as "anti-traditional, progressive, humanist, rationalist, materialist, experimental, individualist, egalitarian, free-thinking and intensely sentimental,"[22] while, in similar vein, Seyyed Hossein Nasr identified four hallmarks of modern thought as anthropomorphism (and by extension secularism), evolutionist progressivism, the absence of any sense of the sacred, and an unrelieved ignorance of metaphysical principles.[23] Sherrard didn't hold back in his repudiation of this modernist frame, which he sheeted home to the triumph of scientism:

> One of the great unresolved psychological enigmas of the modern western world is the question of what or who has persuaded us to accept as virtually axiomatic a self-view and a world-view that demand we reject out of hand the wisdom and vision of our major philosophers and poets in order to imprison our thought and our very selves in the materialist, mechanical, and dogmatic torture-chamber devised by purely quantitative and third-rate scientific minds.[24]

Sherrard mounts a compelling case against an agnostic and materialistic science of nature that had desecrated the world and turned it into a "a vast, smouldering junkyard"; such a science, to be sharply distinguished from traditional sciences, is "a contradiction in terms ... its findings will necessarily correspond to the living reality of nature as little as a corpse corresponds to the living reality of a human being."[25] As Nasr had so forcefully argued in his landmark work *Man and Nature* (1965), the so-called environmental crisis is actually rooted in a spiritual malaise that can only be cured by a return to the wellsprings of Tradition. This would entail an understanding of how the modern worldview had come to exercise its tyrannical grip and how it could be transformed by the Wisdom of the Ages. It was to this task that Sherrard addressed himself in these late works. One of his great contributions was to stress the intimate relationship between the way we view ourselves as human beings and the ways in which we perceive and treat the natural order:

> We do not have any respect, let alone reverence, for the world of nature because we do not have any respect, let alone reverence for ourselves. It is because we cripple and mutilate ourselves that we cripple and mutilate everything else as well. Our contemporary crisis is really our own depravity writ large. . . . Once we repossess a sense of our own holiness, we will recover a sense of the holiness of the world. . . . Only in this way will we once again become aware that our destiny and the destiny of nature are one and the same.[26]

Any proper sense of the natural order depended on a sacramental understanding in which "all that lives is holy" (Blake's phrase, oft-used by Sherrard), all suspended, so to speak, in God. Sherrard often mobilized the insights of the great Christian mystics to help revive this sense, as when he recalls Jan van Ruysbroeck's affirmation of a divine presence in all of creation,

> beyond Time; that is, without before or after, in an Eternal Now. . . the home and beginning of all life and all becoming. And so all creatures are therein, beyond themselves, one being and one Life . . . as in their eternal origin.[27]

Only a renewed sense of the sacred can recover "a sense of our true identity and dignity" as the children of God, made in His image, once again feeling awe and humility, living in nature as "a temple of love and beauty in which we are to worship and adore the Creator." Otherwise we will "proceed headlong along the course to self-destruction to which we are now committed and which is of our own choosing and for which we are entirely responsible." How little we seem to have learned in the three decades and more which have passed since Sherrard wrote these words.

Martin Luther King Jr.

1929–1968

"A drum major for righteousness"

The first principle of value that we need to rediscover is this: that all reality hinges on moral foundations. In other words, that this is a moral universe, and that there are moral laws of the universe just as abiding as the physical laws.[1]

artin Luther King Jr. described Mohendas Gandhi as one of the "individuals who greatly reveal the working of the Spirit of God." The influence of the Mahatma on King's philosophy of nonviolence and its political applications has often been remarked. But it is worth remembering that King came to Gandhi quite late in his own intellectual and moral evolution. The root of his commitment to nonviolence is to be found in Christ's teachings, particularly the Sermon on the Mount, just as Gandhi's understanding was anchored in the ancient religious traditions of India. King defined his identity and purpose in terms of his Christian ministry:

> Before I was a civil rights leader, I was a preacher of the Gospel. This was my first calling and it still remains my greatest commitment. You know, actually all that I do in civil rights I do because I consider it a part of my ministry. I have no other ambitions in life but to achieve excellence in the Christian ministry. I don't plan to run for any political office. I don't plan to do anything but remain a preacher. And what I'm doing in this struggle, along with many others, grows out of my feeling that the preacher must be concerned about the whole man.[2]

King's life, ending on that fateful night in Memphis, is well known and need not be rehearsed here. No appraisal of King's lasting significance in American political history either, or of the many honors he has been afforded since his death. No re-telling of the Montgomery bus boycott or the Birmingham protests or the Selma march, no encomium for the nerve-tingling "I have a dream" speech in Washington (now rivaling Lincoln's Gettysburg Address as the most famous speech in American history), no unravelling of the sordid campaign of vilification by the FBI. No, instead we turn the spotlight onto several interlaced themes running through his writings, sermons, and speeches, and informing all his political activities. We will find many sympathetic resonances between King's Christian commitments and those of many of his companions in the present volume.

Gandhi stood at the forefront of three great revolutions of the era: *against* racism, violence, and colonialism, and *for* unity, peace, and concord. King likewise, but in his case the "colonialism" was not that imposed by a foreign power but by an iniquitous social and economic system that made people of a certain color or class slaves and third-class citizens in their own country. In 1934, at the same time as Gandhi was leading the Indian independence movement, the World Baptist Alliance was meeting in Berlin. This gathering was attended by Martin Luther King Sr., Baptist pastor in Atlanta and early civil rights advocate. Prompted by contemporary developments in Nazi Germany, the WBA issued the following statement:

> This Congress deplores and condemns as a violation of the law of God the Heavenly Father, all racial animosity, and every form of oppression or unfair discrimination toward the Jews, toward colored people, or toward subject races in any part of the world.[3]

The pastor's eldest son inherited not only his name but his understanding of the worldwide, interrelated forms of racism and oppression. Three decades later King Jr. was declaring that "Injustice anywhere is a threat to justice everywhere. We are caught in an inescapable network of mutuality, tied in a single garment of destiny. Whatever affects one directly, affects all indirectly."[4]

There are many possible points of departure for a discussion of King's philosophy but, true to his Christian vocation, the affirmation of the creative and redemptive power of love is perhaps the most appropriate. Here is a characteristic King formulation: "Hatred paralyzes life; love releases it. Hatred confuses life; love harmonizes it. Hatred darkens life; love illuminates it."[5] It was hatred, fueled by fear and ignorance, that was the motive-force of racism, and it was love that seeded King's efforts to combat it. But "love' is a degraded word often signifying little more than a well-intentioned disposition or a sentimental inner glow. To understand its role in King's thought (and indeed in Christian teaching in general) it needs to be linked with several other values—tributaries, it might be said, running into the river of love: humility, courage, self-sacrifice, justice, fidelity to the truth. Let us not forget that in his own lifetime King was a highly controversial figure, reviled, mocked, calumniated as a communist and criminal and conspiracist, hounded by J. Edgar Hoover and the FBI, demonized by the Klu Klux Klan, abused by "black power" hot-heads as an "Uncle Tom," labeled a "demagogue" by Life magazine, his house bombed, his family threatened and terrorized on an almost daily basis, King himself repeatedly harassed, arrested (29 times!), jailed, almost killed in 1958 by a deranged black woman, blackmailed, finally the victim of an assassination that some believe originated in the corridors of power in Washington. Not much room here for easy and empty talk about "love." No, King's love was something sterner, more challenging, more austere, tested in extreme adversity, so often opposed by naked malevolence. The posthumous rehabilitation and idealization of King, sometimes by people and institutions that provided no succour during his lifetime, should not lull us into underestimating the dark forces unleashed by the civil rights movement, nor the many villainies to which King himself was subjected. Instead of retaliating in kind he remained true to his calling:

> As my sufferings mounted I soon realized that there were two ways in which I could respond to my situation—either to react with bitterness or seek to transform the suffering into a creative force. I decided to follow the latter course. . . . The suffering and agonizing moments through which I have passed over the last few years have also drawn me closer to God. More than ever before I am convinced of the reality of a personal God.[6]

How often in these pages have we met with this Christian motif, the transformation of suffering into a creative force. And how unfashionable an idea it is in our own time when the avoidance of pain and the pursuit of comfort and pleasure seem so often to be the order of the day! King continues:

> And I'm not talking about emotional bosh when I talk about love; I'm talking about a strong, demanding love. For I have seen too much hate. I've seen too much hate on the faces of sheriffs in the South. I've seen hate on the faces of too many Klansmen and too many White Citizens Councilors in the South to want to hate, myself, because every time I see it, I know that it does something to their faces and their personalities, and I say to myself that hate is too great a burden to bear. I have decided to love. If you are seeking the highest good, I think you can find it through love. And

the beautiful thing is that we aren't moving wrong when we do it, because John was right, God is love. He who hates does not know God, but he who loves has the key that unlocks the door to the meaning of ultimate reality. . . .[7]

To love is a way of knowing God. In his Nobel Prize speech (1964) King reiterated the "profound moral fact" that should govern the dealings of Christians with their fellows:

> Deeply etched in the fiber of our religious tradition is the conviction that men are made in the image of God and that they are souls of infinite metaphysical value, the heirs of a legacy of dignity and worth. If we feel this as a profound moral fact, we cannot be content to see men hungry, to see men victimized with starvation and ill health when we have the means to help them.

One of Gandhi's formative principles was *satyagraha*, usually translated as "truth-force," sometimes "soul-force": this was the power that is born out of *the marriage of love and truth*. Love answers to the true realities of life, of our existence. In the Mahatma's philosophy and in his political strategies, *satyagraha* must be intertwined with *ahimsa*, usually translated as "nonviolence" but perhaps more precisely as "non-injuriousness," which in turn could only be realized through *brahmacharya*: self-control, without which one would be bereft of the tremendous resolve, strength, and courage which the practice of *satyagraha* and *ahimsa* demanded, and which could only be developed through renunciation and discipline. "*Ahimsa* and truth are so intertwined," said Gandhi, "that it is almost impossible to separate them," while self-discipline provides the basis for their application in daily life. King's vocabulary and moral framework derived from the Christian gospels, but they were altogether consonant with these Gandhian principles. We note in passing that Gandhi himself was deeply influenced by the Sermon on the Mount and acclaimed Jesus as one of history's greatest exponents of *ahimsa*.[8] Gandhi was also influenced by Thoreau's ideas about nonviolence and civil disobedience, as was King. We might also note that King's understanding of ahimsa, in accord with Gandhi's, extended to the animal kingdom, though this was not a theme he ever elaborated beyond stating that "One day the absurdity of the almost universal human belief in the slavery of other animals will be palpable. We shall then have discovered our souls and become worthier of sharing this planet with them."[9] He also shared Gandhi's insistence on the dignity and worth of manual work: "No work is insignificant. All labor that uplifts humanity has dignity and importance and should be undertaken with painstaking excellence."[10]

King's vituperative opponents have made much of his moral foibles, real and imagined, particularly his alleged adultery, which remains unproven but which may well have occurred. Whatever the truth may be, there is no doubt that scandalous rumors about King's behavior were *concocted* and spread about by the FBI, sent to his friends and colleagues, and to his family. Shortly before his assassination, when he was under massive duress, King received a letter that he understood to be motivated by the hope that it would drive him to suicide. At the very least it was intended to drive him out of the leadership of the SCLC (Southern Christian Leadership Conference). It originated in the FBI. In part, this vile letter read,

> The American public, the church organizations that have been helping—Protestants, Catholics, and Jews will know you for what you are—an evil beast. So will others who have backed you. You are done. King, there is only one thing left for you to do. You know what it is… You are done. There is but one way out for you. You better take it before your filthy fraudulent self is bared to the nation.[11]

Readers familiar with the FBI's long history of political chicanery will not be surprised to find it stooping to these squalid depths. Nor will they be startled by later revelations of the CIA's involvement in yet another venal campaign to discredit King. All par for the course really. King resisted this intimidation and blackmail. What should strike us as remarkable is not the fact that King may not have always met the stringent standards of behavior to which he aspired as a Christian pastor—who but the saint never lapses?—but that in the face of so much hostility and bile, so many scurrilous attempts to trash his reputation, he was able to maintain his dignity and—let us not baulk at the word—his *love* for his fellow humans, even his most vicious enemies. Truly remarkable was his willingness "to turn the other cheek" and his posture of forgiveness and conciliation, "not as an occasional act" but as "a constant attitude." An awareness of his own failings no doubt played a part: "There is some good in the worst of us," he wrote, "and some evil in the best of us. When we discover this, we are less prone to hate our enemies."[12] The kind of love King displayed, as did Gandhi before him—and, it might well be said, as did the carpenter from Nazareth—was not driven by sentiment but by moral power:

> Power without love is reckless and abusive, and love without power is sentimental and anemic. Power at its best is love implementing the demands of justice, and justice at its best is power correcting everything that stands against love.[13]

Like Gandhi, King understood that means and ends are inseparable, that noble ends cannot be achieved by base means.

> Darkness cannot drive out darkness: only light can do that. Hate cannot drive out hate: only love can do that.[14]

> Peace is not merely a distant goal that we seek, but a means by which we arrive at that goal.[15]

> So I have tried to make it clear that it is wrong to use immoral means to attain moral ends. But now I must affirm that it is just as wrong, or even more so, to use moral means to preserve immoral ends.[16]

The demands of truth required that King's fellow-Americans confront a long history of blood-soaked racist injustice, visited not only on Afro-Americans but on the continent's oldest inhabitants:

> Our nation was born in genocide when it embraced the doctrine that the original American, the Indian, was an inferior race. Even before there were large numbers of Negroes on our shore, the scar of racial hatred had already disfigured colonial society. From the sixteenth century forward, blood flowed in battles over racial supremacy. We are perhaps the only nation which tried as a matter of national policy to wipe out its indigenous population. Moreover, we elevated that tragic experience into a noble crusade. Indeed, even today we have not permitted ourselves to reject or feel remorse for this shameful episode. Our literature, our films, our drama, our folklore all exalt it. Our children are still taught to

respect the violence which reduced a red-skinned people of an earlier culture into a few fragmented groups herded into impoverished reservations.[17]

This confrontation with the truth of a national history saturated in violence and injustice is one that many Americans are, apparently, still unwilling to face. (The same, sadly, can be said of many Australians.) As James Baldwin somewhere tersely observed, "Not everything that is faced can be changed, but nothing can be changed until it is faced." King believed that ultimately truth and love would triumph: "I believe that unarmed truth and unconditional love will have the final word in reality. This is why right, temporarily defeated, is stronger than evil triumphant."[18] "The moral arc of the universe," he famously declared, "is long but it bends towards justice."[19] But until that time of self-reckoning American society cannot be "a society at peace with itself, a society that can live with its conscience." King was also fully aware of the problems posed by ostensibly sympathetic advocates of "moderation" and "gradualism" and "compromise," as he so eloquently and painfully stated in *Letter from Birmingham Jail* (1963) addressed to his fellow-ministers and to rabbis:

> I must make two honest confessions to you, my Christian and Jewish brothers. First, I must confess that over the past few years I have been gravely disappointed with the white moderate. I have almost reached the regrettable conclusion that the Negro's great stumbling block in his stride toward freedom is not the White Citizen's Councilor or the Ku Klux Klanner, but the white moderate, who is more devoted to "order" than to justice; who prefers a negative peace which is the absence of tension to a positive peace which is the presence of justice; who constantly says: "I agree with you in the goal you seek, but I cannot agree with your methods of direct action"; who paternalistically believes he can set the time-table for another man's freedom; who lives by a mythical concept of time and who constantly advises the Negro to wait for a "more convenient season." Shallow understanding from people of good will is more frustrating than absolute misunderstanding from people of ill will. Lukewarm acceptance is much more bewildering than outright rejection.

At a time when, in some quarters, the whole concept of "race" (always a potent, highly problematic and unstable term) has fallen prey to the totalizing discourse of "critical race theory" and its many attendant inanities and hostilities, it is salutary to remember that King's campaign against racism took its bearing from very different sources. It might also be incidentally observed that "critical race theory" sometimes perpetrates forms of racism in its own proponents, albeit in a fashion that is unintended and unconscious, thus subverting its own avowed ends—but that's a subject for another day. Nor should we forget that racism, in King's view, was imbricated with all manner of other factors—class stratifications, the exploitative and destructive dynamics of capitalism, American exceptionalism, militarism, and imperialism. So, for instance, King writes,

> one day we must ask the question, "Why are there forty million poor people in America?" And when you begin to ask that question, you are raising questions about the economic system, about a broader distribution of wealth. When you ask that question, you begin to question the capitalistic economy.[20]

Similarly, King, encouraged by the Vietnamese monk Thich Nhat Hanh, publicly voiced his opposition to America's military intervention in Vietnam, a stand that alienated many folk who had hitherto supported his campaign for civil rights. Others argued that his public opposition to the war was deflecting attention from the civil rights issue, as if standing up against one evil might defraud another just cause. In his now-famous speech, "Beyond Vietnam: A Time to Break the Silence" (April, 1967), King linked the anti-war cause to global economic injustices in which America was deeply implicated:

> A true revolution of values will soon look uneasily on the glaring contrast of poverty and wealth. With righteous indignation, it will look across the seas and see individual capitalists of the West investing huge sums of money in Asia, Africa, and South America, only to take the profits out with no concern for the social betterment of the countries, and say: "This is not just."

For King, injustice, whatever its form, must be resisted. From late in his life:

I'm concerned about a better world. I'm concerned about justice; I'm concerned about brotherhood; I'm concerned about truth. And when one is concerned about that, he can never advocate violence.[21]

Early in this discussion we noted King's steadfast dedication to his vocation as a Christian minister. At the time of his death he was still serving, with his father, as co-pastor of the Ebenezer Baptist Church in Atlanta. He was true to the ideal he had affirmed and pursued throughout: "The end of life is not to be happy, nor to achieve pleasure and avoid pain, but to do the will of God, come what may."

James Cowan

1942–2018

Explorations in Time, Space and the Beyond

*My task has always been to revive the concept of numen…
to alert readers to a state of reverence present in all things.*[1]

espite the publication of some forty or so books, James Cowan remains a prophet without honor in his own country. This is partly of his own doing. He spent many years living elsewhere. His early interest in colonial settlement and then in Aboriginal culture eventually gave way to explorations more remote in both time and space. When, in later years, he did return to Australia he evinced little appetite for the kinds of involvements that might have brought him more local recognition from both scholars and the writers' festival crowd. He didn't mind being unfashionable, but he would no doubt have appreciated a more sympathetic audience in a country in which he had traveled so widely and about which he had written many fine books. His death in 2018 remained unremarked in the modish forums of the literary establishment. The fact that he garnered much more recognition and respect overseas than he did in Australia should embarrass us.

Late in life Cowan wrote a brief *credo*:

> Throughout my life as a writer I have tried to find a way to serve the rights and aspirations of indigenous peoples, and what their perspective means to the modern world. I have also tried to reaffirm the ancient spiritual canon of the West. Our saints and our philosophers are our greatest supernatural asset. We should honor their perennial place among us. And finally, nature is our mistress. We should preserve her integrity whenever she is demeaned by those forces of utility that threaten her very existence. Protecting her bill-of-rights is a lifelong task of mine.[2]

But before discussing his enduring concerns, a truncated account of a rich and adventurous life. As I was lucky enough to know him as a friend in the last two years of his life I allow myself the liberty of referring to him as James. In any case, he was not a fellow to stand on formalities.

James was born in Melbourne in the war years but spent most of his childhood in Castlecrag, on the northern arm of Sydney Harbor, where he nurtured an early love of the coastal and bush landscapes. Holiday excursions to his grandfather's property on the Murray River quickened his interest in colonial settlement and rural life.[3] His father, an air force navigator during the war, took up a position with Qantas, sparking James's lifelong interest in aviation. When I enquired how he supported himself when his book royalties were running thin during the years he was living in Europe and North Africa, he replied, with characteristic insouciance, "Oh that was no problem Harry. I would organize tours, charter a plane, load it up with wealthy tourists and take them into the North African desert."

Studies at Sydney University galvanized his reading, particularly the modernist avant-garde—Baudelaire, Rimbaud, de Nerval, Pound, and the like. James was nursing an ambition to become a writer. He was always in love with words: "All my life I have lived among words, from my first library book to the cryptic carvings of myths on bamboo wafers tied together by a Balinese priest. Words have long congregated in the corridors of my mind. Adventitious text, the promulgation of stories as the first step towards understanding."[4] In 1964 he published Nine Poems in Mauritius, where his father was stationed at that time, one of the many exotic places where James pitched his tent. As a young man James trod a well-beaten track for aspiring litterateurs: Tahiti, Canada, New York, London, Paris, and Greece, where he contracted tuberculosis, prompting a return to Australia for convalescence. The next two decades were given over to his time-and-space explorations of his homeland. His far-reaching travels included a two-year sojourn in Balgo Hills, a remote Aboriginal settlement in the Tanami Desert, where he and his wife, Wendy, helped to establish the Warlayirti Artists Cooperative, soon a thriving business enterprise. In the mid-90s he returned to Europe to live in Italy for three years and thence to Argentina. About fifteen years ago, trying to contact James about including a piece of his writing in an anthology I was editing, I had the devil's own job locating him. None of his many publishers knew where he was. I eventually tracked him down in Buenos Aires.[5] The last years of his life were spent in Queensland and north-eastern NSW. He died in 2018. Shortly before his death he wrote, "the drums on outer islands replicate the sounds of the earth. They are calling to me, these skin-covered, hollowed-out logs shaped liked charging horns, urging me to heed their voices… They are calling to me across the waters."[6]

James was a prolific writer in many different genres: eight novels, one of which, *The Mapmaker's Dream* (1996), secured his international reputation; five volumes of poetry; three large-format illustrated books in collaboration with photographer Colin Beard, about the early history of European settlement in Australia (*The Mountain Men, The River People, Starlight's Trail*), another a compendium of indigenous sacred sites all over the continent (*Sacred Places in Australia*); three monographs about Aboriginal art; translations of Persian and Indian poetry; four collections of essays; five books about Christian scriptures, saints, and mystics; children's literature; a biography of the colorful Renaissance figure Vespasiano Gonzaga (earning him a doctorate from Queensland University); and, most importantly, half-a-dozen books about the myths, cosmology, rituals, and esoteric life of the Aborigines and other non-literate peoples. Over the years he spent time living with many indigenous folk who remained largely untouched by the modern world: the Tuareg of the Sahara, the Berbers in Morocco, the Iban of Borneo, Torres Strait islanders, the first peoples of his homeland. He also stayed in ancient Christian monasteries in the Biblical lands of the Middle East and North Africa. Many of his writings were germinated by these wanderings, each book "a voyage or quest for meaning and insight, a journey that draws attention to a spiritual quality that has been lost or endangered by the nihilism of modernity."[7] As fellow-Australian author Jill Ker Conway has written, "his visual sense, and his capacity for entering into the sensibility of traditional peoples, makes his work an aesthetic and intellectual adventure." James was a man of insatiable curiosity, prodigious energy, and infectious enthusiasm, dedicated to the life of the mind, to the craft of writing, and to the exploration of the world's most remote places and peoples—adventures of body, mind, and spirit, a lifelong pilgrimage. James found his final resting-place in the Orthodox Church, to which he had been attracted since early adulthood. He continued working until just a few weeks before he crossed to the "Other-side Camp," as the Native Americans call our post-mortem destination. The last time I heard from him he sent a typescript of his latest work, The Book of Letters, meditations on each letter of the alphabet with captivating musings about petroglyphs, scripts, hieroglyphs, symbols of all kinds, the mysteries of language.[8] As his friend Peter Thompson has written, "James Cowan's life was that of a poet, a single-minded pursuit of perennial truth, and the fashioning of a clear, stripped-back style devoid, as he said, of the old mechanisms of literary realism."

Before turning to some aspects of James's work, perhaps I might be permitted a personal anecdote. I first met James face-to-face when he invited me to Byron Bay to deliver a talk on the Lakota sage and visionary, Black Elk. For some time, James had been the prime mover in a community group, Café Philo, where people met to hear talks and discuss matters of philosophical and spiritual moment. Later that year, despite ill-health, James and his wife came to my hometown, Bendigo, where James was enthused by the rich local history and the colonial architecture. During this visit he suffered a severe attack which had him at death's door. He was rushed to hospital in the middle of the night. We were told that his condition was extremely grave. I sat at his bedside for several hours in the far reaches of the night, alarmed by the demeanor of the doctors who flitted in and out, and by James's own pallid appearance and acute pain. But whenever I pressed inquiries about his state, he impatiently brushed these aside. He was intent on telling me, in some detail and with more excitement than was good for him, about two previously unknown letters from Michelangelo that he had discovered during his Renaissance researches in Italy. Later that year, not long before his death, I visited James in Bangalow. Despite his physical affliction and obvious frailty he remained eager to discuss all sorts of subjects of mutual interest. I recall, among many other things, his lively discourse on René Daumal's mystical novel *Mount Analogue*, reminiscences about the Aboriginal elder "Sunfly" who figures prominently in *Two Men Dreaming,* his half-serious and amusing diatribes about publishers, ruminations on Christ as Pantocrator, and his recollections of various well-known people whom he had encountered in many parts of the world—the most impressive of whom, he said, was the English poet and Blake scholar, Kathleen Raine. We also shared an abiding interest in the work of the great perennialists, principally René Guénon and Ananda Coomaraswamy.

James was one of the few people with whom I have felt able to discuss my spiritual life without any self-consciousness. I was deeply moved by his account of his attraction to Orthodox Christology and mystical theology, and his commitment to the Eastern Church. He had been impelled thither for many of the same reasons as had Philip Sherrard, whom we met earlier in this volume.[9] In an interview for Inner Explorations publications, James discusses his many visits to ancient chapels and monasteries in the Balkans, North Africa, and the Middle East, dating back to the 1960s:

> [The attraction to Eastern Orthodoxy] happened very early in my life.... I soon came to realize that I was dealing with a subtle knowledge that my Western Christian upbringing had not alluded to. Eastern Orthodoxy does not look to hierarchy, or to Church dogma, in order to bolster its view of the spirit. Rather, it is permeated by a subtle essence that is derived from humankind's willingness to embrace metaphor as its bridge to the other world. Metaphysics is a real science in the East, I discovered. When I read of Gregory Palamas' doctrine of gnosial knowledge in the form of *hesychia,* or, let's call it, "indwellment in stillness," I realized that this was what I had been missing all my life. Christianity did have a clear view on mystical knowledge that was not wedded to ethics, as it is so often in Western Christian doctrine. It reminded me of Zen Buddhism and yogi practice.

After talking about the spiritual sustenance he received from the *Philokalia* and from the example of figures such as St Antony and St Francis (the subjects of two of his books), James goes on to say

> Western Christianity is deeply grounded in the legalisms of Catholicism and the reliance on conscience as we see in Protestantism. Nestorianism, the Coptic Church, and Greek Orthodoxy are grounded in a more mystical view of spirituality that to the West may well contain residual heresies, but this is not the point. They work. They allow a person to tap into a more subtle view of things.[10]

The novel *A Mapmaker's Dream* (1996) gave James an international profile as well as a welcome income stream. It was his only book that caused a real splash in Australia, awarded the Australian Literature Society's Gold Medal. Of his eight novels, the best of the rest is probably *A Troubadour's Testament* (1998), in the same vein. James set great store on his literary accomplishments as a novelist, poet, and essayist, and was indefatigable in striving after a style that would fuse a mythopoeic sensibility with modernist literary strategies. He loved talking about such things. But the world is full of clever and sophisticated writers. For my own part, I do not believe that this is where James made his most durable contribution as a writer. In fact I have to say that his literary output was patchy, some of it downright bad. His corpus of non-fictional/poetic work is, in the main, impressive and wide-ranging. Here was a man who could write with equal facility—a double-edged word I use advisedly—about Australian bush lore, Parmenidean metaphysics, computer technology, Ibn Arabi, and the erotic poetry of ancient India. Consider the subjects he covers in just one of his collections of essays, *A Spanner in the Works: Science and the Spiritual Life* (2007): pre-Socratic philosophy, archaic science, medieval theology and mysticism, Renaissance art, the scientific theories of Max Planck and Einstein, Walter Benjamin, the life of Simone Weil, the contemporary information overload... It was a collection of which his friend, the American scholar Arthur Versluis, wrote this:

> In A Spanner in the Works, the inimitable James Cowan—master of incandescent fiction, and explorer of exotic lands of the spirit—reflects on artistic and scientific achievement, and on how, in the flatland of modernity, we can recover a sense of the poetic, the heroic, and the mythic. Erudite, provocative, these are essays to be savored.[11]

James's work on Christian saints and mystics provided another meeting ground for his philosophical and literary proclivities. These works are lively, often charming, somewhat idiosyncratic, always attuned to Karen Armstrong's excellent dictum that "a theology should be like poetry, which takes us to the end of what words and thoughts can do." It should also be said that James sometimes fashioned historical figures in his own image. Peter Mathews has noted this tendency in both the fictional and non-fictional works:

> Cowan subordinates his subjects to his own philosophical presuppositions, lacing them with themes and motives that derive from the turn of the twenty-first century and mistaking them for eternal

ideas. Saint Francis... is not a Kierkegaardian knight of faith, looking to suspend the march of world history: such an idea is the product of nineteenth-century European philosophy, and as such is completely alien to the time in which Francis lived. Yet Cowan maps his own desires and values onto Francis's life, transforming him into a modern existentialist hero.[12]

To my mind, his most significant achievement was the elucidation of traditional Aboriginal culture, which was the living expression, the incarnation we might say, of a primordial birthright vouchsafed by the multivalent term, the Dreaming.

There are several factors which made James's contribution to Aboriginal Studies highly distinctive, in some respects unique. Firstly, James brought to his inquiries a mind steeped in the "high culture" of Western Europe, stretching back to Antiquity, *and* permeated by his lived experiences with nomadic and indigenous peoples in many parts of the world. He was simultaneously adventurer, scholar, and seeker. Secondly, he was familiar with the vast storehouse of anthropological data on the Aborigines, and had assimilated the most lasting insights of the more sympathetic anthropologists of earlier times; we may mention figures such as T. G. Strehlow, R. H. Mathews and especially A. P. Elkin whose pioneering work on "Aboriginal men of high degree" concerned the arcane domain in which James was most interested.[13] But he was never constricted by the methods and protocols of academic writing, bringing to his work an existential engagement and a poet's imaginative powers. As Kathleen Raine remarked of his work in this field, "James Cowan brings with him quite another kind of understanding." As James himself stated quite unequivocally, "It is plainly evident that this confinement of the exploration of Aboriginal culture to the academic environment has led to a malnourished vision of what Aboriginal spirituality is all about... genuine intellectual intuition has been replaced by scholastic techniques masquerading as 'social science.'" Thirdly, James was thoroughly versed in the perennial philosophy, which provided him with an adequate metaphysical and cosmological framework of which nearly all anthropologists were, and are, completely bereft. Without the insights of writers like René Guénon, Ananda Coomaraswamy, Henry Corbin, and Mircea Eliade, James would not have been able to write about Aboriginal tradition with such insight. One need only recall chapter titles like "The Metaphysics of Space," "Landscape as Metaphor," "Nature as Numen," or ponder such affirmations as these:

> To apprehend a spiritual life, one must first acknowledge the absolute existence of a metaphysical reality that is as substantive as the one we know as the so-called physical reality.... Our age has slipped away from recognizing a metaphysical reality.

> Mytho-poetry is one of the supreme talents of humankind. We must make sure that its flame never dies out.... Myth is the supreme metaphysical language.

> Recognizing the Dreaming as a living reality . . . demands a shift in the attitudes of everyone concerned. It requires, firstly, that the Dreaming is seen for what it is: a metaphysical statement about the origins of mankind as a spiritual being.

Then too, for James, the preservation of primordial wisdom was not only related to his own personal quest but was a matter of the most profound and urgent global import: "It is my belief that without the world's oldest spiritual heritages the world will soon wither and die at its root." Unlike many of the more sentimental commentators who give a glib and now-fashionable acquiescence to such formulations, James meant this quite literally and in all seriousness: *the fate of the world*, he insisted, *depends on the preservation of these wisdom traditions.* He said so many times. "It is not traditional man that will die out when the last Aborigine or Sioux or Kalahari Bushman quits the earth; it will be the spirit of man as nature's consort that will finally disappear."[14]

James's providential encounters in the Australian outback with several elders, including "Big Bill" Neidjie[15] and Sunfly, provided him with a precious if precarious link to a way of life that was fast disappearing under the onslaughts of the modern world. The rare testimony of men such as Sunfly was disclosed in a context quite different from that of the anthropological expeditions of the nineteenth and early twentieth centuries. Here we might note a marked contrast with the literature on the spiritual heritage of the North American Indians, where there is a rich deposit of personal histories from many individuals still well-versed in the old ways, recorded by people with the same sort of sensitive receptivity that James brought to his work. One thinks of such invaluable documents as *Black Elk Speaks* by John Neihardt, *The Sacred Pipe* by Joseph Epes Brown, *Lame Deer, Seeker of Visions* by Richard Erdoes, the several works of Luther Standing Bear, Michael Fitzgerald's *Yellowtail: Crow Medicine Man and Sundance Chief.*[16] For reasons too complex to unravel here, there is no comparable literature in Australia. A melancholy fact. Against this backdrop we must be all the more grateful for James's intrepid efforts to find the few remaining custodians of an ancient wisdom and the last witnesses of a way of life that had disappeared in all but the most remote and inaccessible parts of Australia. While all of his writings about primal cultures vibrate with shimmering insights, his single most important book in this field is *Mysteries of the Dream-time*, along with the more autobiographical *Two Men Dreaming*.

In recent years James's work in the domain of Aboriginal Studies has come under some fire, particularly from indigenous scholar Mitchell Rolls, whose critique deserves to be heard and considered —but this is beyond our present ambit; I only opine that some of the critique, as it relates to the overheated and vexatious subject of "cultural appropriation," seems to me to be quite captious and counter-productive.[17] Given the scandalous Australian neglect of James's writings, I suppose one might be half-grateful that his work is at least attracting some attention even if it is sometimes mis-guided. Whatever may have been his unconscious motivations (and anyhow, who would know?), and whatever may have been the shortcomings of his work, without James Cowan our knowledge— "our" in its fullest sense—would be greatly impoverished. The least we can do is make an appropriate if belated acknowledgement.

James Cowan: Select Bibliography

On Aboriginal and Other Primal Traditions
Mysteries of the Dream-time (1989)
Sacred Places in Australia (1991)
Letters from a Wild State (1991)

The Elements of the Aborigine Tradition (1992)
Messengers of the Gods: Tribal Elders Reveal the Ancient Wisdom of the Earth (1993)
Myths of the Dreaming: Interpreting Aboriginal Legends (1994)
Two Men Dreaming: A Memoir, A Journey (1995)

On Christian Tradition

Journey to the Inner Mountain: In the Desert with St. Antony (2001)
Francis: a Saint's Way (2002)
Quartet: Four Essays on Power (2006)
   (on Boethius, Maximos the Confessor, John of the Cross and Suhrawardi)
The Deposition (a novel) (2008)
Fleeing Herod: Through Egypt with the Holy Family (2013)
The Book with No Name (2019)
   (on the *Evangelicum Longum*)

Marilynne Robinson

1943–

Gilead and a Sense of Wonder

Christianity is a life, not a doctrine…

arilynne Robinson was born in 1943 IN modest circumstances in Standpoint, Idaho. In 2004 she published her second novel, *Gilead*. In the intervening years she lived a quiet and comparatively obscure life. University studies took to her to Pembroke College (an adjunct of Brown University, Rhode Island) where she distinguished herself as a student of literature, later earning a PhD at the University of Washington. In 1967 she married and had two sons. She and her husband separated some years later. She was raised as a Presbyterian but, attracted by the theology of John Calvin, she became a Congregationalist and an occasional preacher. Her first published novel, *Housekeeping*, appeared in 1980, followed by *Mother Country: Britain, the Welfare State and Nuclear Pollution* (1989) and *The Death of Adam: Essays on Modern Thought* (1998). In 1991 she joined the faculty of the University of Iowa as a teacher of literature and creative writing. During these years she attained some recognition in literary and academic circles. In 2005 she found herself in the limelight when she won the Pulitzer Prize for *Gilead*, a novel of wondrous beauty with an unlikely protagonist, an elderly Congregationalist minister in his dying days, living in a small (fictional) town in Iowa. Three novels with interconnecting narratives have followed to give us a tetralogy that will ensure Robinson a lofty place in American letters. "Her novels are replete with a sense of felt life, with a deep and abiding sympathy for her characters and a full understanding of their inner lives."[1] Robinson has also published several more compilations of her provocative and searching essays, lectures, and sermons. She retired from her position at the University of Iowa in 2016. In recent years, showered with awards, she has become an unlikely and, one suspects, reluctant media celebrity, appearing on the Oprah Winfrey Show, joining President Barack Obama in a broadcast conversation in 2015, and being frequently subjected to interviews by journalists, academics, and cultural commentators.

I first encountered Robinson's work when I read *Gilead*, soon after its publication. I was thrilled and deeply moved, as I was later by *Home* and *Lila*. (The most recent novel, *Jack*, I found less enthralling for reasons that need not detain us here.) *Gilead*, in my reckoning, is the finest American novel of the last half-century, gently nudging out other contenders such as Cormac McCarthy's *All the Pretty Horses*, *Stoner* by John Williams, and Wallace Stegner's *The Angle of Repose*. I am altogether in agreement with Ann Patchett's lovely encomium:

> Gilead is a book that deserves to be read slowly, thoughtfully, and repeatedly.... I would like to see copies of it dropped onto pews across our country, where it could sit among the Bibles and hymnals and collection envelopes. It would be a good reminder of what it means to lead a noble and moral life—and, for that matter, what it means to write a truly great novel.[2]

Some of the attractions of Robinson's work are obvious enough. As a novelist she writes in a quiet voice with rare grace, beauty, and power; as an essayist she is deeply thoughtful, robust, and incisive. Her prose ripples with beautiful Biblical cadences and allusions, and often brings the Psalms to mind—the gravity, the beauty, the sense of awe, the thanks-giving. Sometimes she moves towards the epigrammatic without ever becoming sophistic or oracular or pontifical. A sample:

> Every sorrow suggests a thousand songs, and every song recalls a thousand sorrows, and so they are infinite in number, and all the same.

> Love is holy because it is like grace—the worthiness of its object is never really what matters.

> The eternal as an idea is much less preposterous than time, and this very fact should seize our attention.

> Nothing true about God can be said from a posture of defense.

> Prayer is a discipline in truthfulness, in honesty.

> The force behind the movement of time is a mourning that will not be comforted.[3]

In a fine essay in the *New Yorker* Mark O'Connell wrote that

> There is nothing fraudulent about her eloquence, nothing remotely shifty or meretricious about the beauty of her sentences. Her voice is at once sad and ecstatic, conversationally fluent and

formally precise. And it doesn't feel like a performance or a feint. It doesn't feel like vanity . . . it feels like wisdom.[4]

Robinson's corpus as a whole is well beyond our reach here, but her work, not only as a novelist but as a culture critic, philosopher, and theologian, deserves the most serious and sustained attention. She has written many wise words on all sorts of subjects, including environmental disaster, tribal politics, education, Darwinism, literature, Marx, the Bible, the nuclear spectre, Freud, liberalism... an inquiring, supple, generous, and capacious mind at work. Her outlook is of a conservative cast, not in the narrow partisan-political sense but in its rootedness in the past. I am put in mind of Wendell Berry's well-seasoned observation that

> Contemporaneity, in the sense of being "up with the times," is of no value. Wakefulness to experience—as well as to instruction and example—is another matter. But what we call the modern world is not necessarily, and not often, the real world, and there is no virtue in being up-to-date in it.[5]

I daresay this is one reason why Robinson does not own a television set. Not the least of her many accomplishments is her recuperation, both in fiction and in her nuanced philosophical and theological discourses, of the Calvinist ideal;[6] could any project be more unfashionable! As a reviewer of *The Death of Adam* wrote, "We all know that the Puritans were dour, sex-hating, joy-abominating folk— except that, as Robinson shows, this widely embraced caricature is a calumny."[7]

Here I want simply to ponder a few passages from *Gilead* that give us intimations of Robinson's religious sensibility and her fine-grained moral seriousness. The novel is set in 1956 in Gilead; its name, Robinson later tells us, means "hill of witness." She has also called it a "dogged outpost," one depicted with a quiet but clear-eyed affection. ("To play catch on an evening, to smell the river, to hear the train pass. These little towns were once the bold ramparts meant to shelter just such peace.") The novel is cast in epistolary form, narrated by the dying John Ames, seventy-six years old, looking back over three generations of troubled family history and over his own long and mostly lonely life. Ames's wife dies during the birth of their first child, as does the infant. Many long years later Ames marries again, and now has a seven-year-old son. The old minister's ruminations comprise a kind of last testament addressed to his son, a distillation of what he has seen and experienced and learned. Much of the poignancy of the story derives from Ames's sense (and ours) of the gap between a life just starting and one soon to end. While it is perilous to identify an author's views with those of her characters, we may suppose—supported by the tenor of the rest of Robinson's *oeuvre*—that Ames is in large measure a conduit for the author's own vision of life. Let's bring into the foreground view four leitmotifs, flagged by four simple words, but each with a strong Christian inflexion: suffering, love, grace, and wonder.

Ames has experienced and shared much *suffering* in his life: loneliness, the legacies of violence and jealousy and malice, the burden of a troubled family history, the ravages of guilt, the pain of relationships rooted in "mutual incomprehension." He is on intimate terms with the dark side of human nature, both through his personal history and through his vocation as a pastor. "Man is born to trouble as the sparks fly upward," he says. One of his abiding concerns is with the psychic corrosions of guilt: "It has been my experience that guilt can burst through the smallest breach and cover the landscape, and abide in it in pools and danknesses, just as native as water." So, here is a bitter datum of human experience: life is full of sadness and sorrow, of sin and suffering, of affliction, of misunderstanding, of loneliness and grief. We are "fallen" beings living in an imperfect world. No room for Pollyannas, no room for sentimentalists of any kind in the world of John Ames (or of John Calvin or Marilynne Robinson). *But* suffering is not meaningless. "What is the purpose of a prophet," asks Ames, "except to find meaning in trouble?"—as he does in his own trials: "I am grateful for all those dark years, even though in retrospect they seem like a long, bitter prayer that was answered finally." Here is a striking passage that brings to mind Dostoevsky and Weil and, indeed, Christian thought in general. It will stick in the craw of many progressivists, reformers, believers in human "perfectibility," the epigones of Rousseau and Marx, all revolutionaries and Utopians:

My faith tells me that God shared poverty, suffering, and death with human beings, which can only mean that such things are full of dignity and meaning, even though to believe this makes a great demand on one's faith, and to act as if this were true in any way we understand is to be ridiculous. It is ridiculous also to act as if it were not absolutely and essentially true all the same.

"Suffering redeemed by *love*," a refrain in Robinson's work, is a theme we have already met many times in the present volume. Love, in its fullest Christian sense and stripped of all of its sentimental accretions, is the working of Divine love through the human person; it is, in William Law's words, "heaven revealed in the soul; it is light and truth . . . it has no errors for all errors are the want of love." And so, for the Christian, God's love for us, made manifest in Christ, our love of God, and our love of our neighbor, are all part of a seamless whole. But to state the case in such bald terms is to reduce the reality of this love, to strip it of its mystery, of its revelatory power, for love on the human plane is "only a glimpse or parable of an embracing, incomprehensible reality . . . the eternal breaking in on the temporal." In one of his essays Frithjof Schuon, perennialist metaphysician-philosopher, affirms that "A spiritual virtue is nothing other than a consciousness of a reality."[8] Robinson, I think, would agree, as she would with Augustine's claim that "the love of God comprises all virtues." For Robinson, writing fiction can in itself be "an exercise in the capacity for imaginative love, or sympathy, or identification."[9]

One of the less attractive aspects latent in American Puritanism—these days on all too frequent display in aberrant pseudo-religious forms—is a censorious and punitive moralism, the harsh and often hypocritical judgment of the moral failure of others; the shadow, so to speak, of the stringent Puritan insistence on moral probity. To apply the most testing standards to one's own behavior is an estimable hallmark of the Puritan ethos, embodied in Ames himself; to judge others, however, is to betray one of Christ's own injunctions. So it is that Ames insists that "the grace of God is sufficient to any transgression, and that to judge is wrong, the origin and essence of much error and cruelty." The refusal to judge is one expression of love.

God's love working in the world: *grace.* Every human situation, every human encounter, gives us an opportunity to share in this grace:

> When you encounter another person, when you have dealings with anyone at all, it is as if a question is being put to you. So you must think, What is the Lord asking of me in this moment, in this situation? If you confront insult or antagonism, your first impulse will be to respond in kind. But if you think, as it were, This is an emissary sent from the Lord, and some benefit is intended for me, first of all the occasion to demonstrate my faithfulness, *the chance to show that I do in some small degree participate in the grace that saved me,* you are free to act otherwise than as circumstances would seem to dictate. You are free to act by your own lights. You are freed at the same time of the impulse to hate or resent that person [italics mine].

An immersion in suffering, love, and grace engenders a sacramental sense of *wonder*, a reverential posture in relation to God, to all His creatures, to the whole creation, a sense of the sacred. Life is never free of suffering and perplexity, but it is also full of beauty. As Ames says, "There is more beauty than our eyes can bear, precious things have been put into our hands and to do nothing to honor them is to do great harm." We find this sense of wonder in many of the finest American writers, in the nature writing of Emerson, Thoreau, and Muir, the poetry of Whitman, the novels of Willa Cather, the poems and essays of Wendell Berry. It is also powerfully present in some of the work of film-maker Terrence Malick, who entitles one of his films *To the Wonder* (unhappily, one of his least impressive films). In Robinson's case I think this sense of wonder, which we might just as easily call reverence, is most movingly expressed through her depictions of the singularity of each human person, each human soul.

> Any human face is a claim on you, because you can't help but understand the singularity of it, the courage and loneliness of it. But this is truest of the face of an infant. I consider that to be one kind of vision, as mystical as any.

She would no doubt endorse the words of the Psalmist, "I will give thanks unto thee, for I am fearfully and wonderfully made: marvelous are thy works, and that my soul knoweth right well" (Psalm 139:14). A sense of wonder also suffuses her evocations of the natural world. Here are two characteristic excerpts from *Gilead*:

> I love the prairie! So often I have seen the dawn come and the light flood over the land and everything turn radiant at once, that word "good" so profoundly affirmed in my soul that I am amazed I should be allowed to witness such a thing. There may have been a more wonderful first moment "when the morning stars sang together and all the sons of God shouted for joy," but for all I know to the contrary, they still do sing and shout, and they certainly might well. Here on the prairie there is nothing to distract attention from the evening and the morning, nothing on the horizon to abbreviate or to delay. Mountains would seem an impertinence from that point of view.

> The sun had come up brilliantly after a heavy rain, and the trees were glistening and very wet. On some impulse, plain exuberance, I suppose, the fellow jumped up and caught hold of a branch, and a storm of luminous water came pouring down on the two of them, and they laughed and took off running, the girl sweeping water off her hair and her dress as if she were a little bit disgusted, but she wasn't. It was a beautiful thing to see, like something from a myth. I don't know why I thought of that now, except perhaps because it is easy to believe in such moments that water was made primarily for blessing, and only secondarily for growing vegetables or doing the wash. I wish I had paid more attention to it.

As well as highlighting these Christian melodies in *Gilead* I want to stress one other theme in Robinson's writings, present but somewhat muted in the novel, foregrounded in her philosophical and theological writing. I have found no reference to Simone Weil in Robinson's writings, but the French mystic, it seems to me, beautifully articulated the novelist's position on the issue at hand. It is worth repeating: "The mysteries of faith are degraded if they are made into an object of affirmation and negation, when in reality they should be an object of contemplation" (from *Gravity and Grace*). This is to say, as Robinson often *does* say, that rational argument about God and His ways, has its proper place, but it can only take us a small way and, indeed, when disputatious, can often be a distraction that "unsettles" faith. Ames again: "So my advice is this—don't look for proofs. Don't bother with them at all. They are never sufficient to the question, and they're always a little impertinent, I think, because they claim for God a place within our conceptual grasp." And similarly, "I'm not going to force some theory on a mystery and make foolishness of it, just because that is what people who talk about it normally do." However, all this notwithstanding, it would be foolishness of another kind to underestimate Robinson's own gift both for religious discourse and for puncturing the shibboleths of the modern outlook, particularly in its more self-congratulatory forms, one of which is the tedious celebration of its own self-proclaimed "liberation" from religious "superstitions." If the metaphor were not so belligerent one would be tempted to say that she has administered a fair shirtfront on the likes of Richard Dawkins, Steven Pinker, and Christopher Hitchens. (In any case, how seriously can we take these chaps when they write books with titles like *Enlightenment Now* and *Outgrowing God*?) No one who has read *Absence of Mind* or *The Death of Adam* will be in any doubt about Robinson's formidable intellectual powers or her moral alertness. Reviewing *The Absence of Mind*, the eminent writer on religious subjects, Karen Armstrong, properly wrote of this intervention in the contemporary debate about "science" and "religion," "Robinson's argument is prophetic, profound, eloquent, succinct, powerful and timely."[10]

I refer finally to one of the other delights of reading *Gilead*, and indeed all of Robinson's work: her capacity to *surprise* us. It might be a turn of phrase, a startling insight quietly presented, a fugitive impression, a modest but perfectly turned apophthegm. Here is one example, from Ames's reveries, which I particularly like:

> I have always wondered if the Commandments should be read as occurring in order of importance. If that is correct, honoring your mother is more important than not committing murder. That seems remarkable, though I am open to the idea.

In *No Man is an Island*, Thomas Merton writes that "All true art . . . makes us alive to the tremendous mystery of being, in which we ourselves, together with all other living things and existing things, come forth from the depths of God and return again to Him. An art that does not produce something of this is not worth the name."[11] Robinson's art is certainly worthy of the name.

Aleksandr Isayevich Solzhenitsyn

1918–2008

"A permanent, earnest duty"

The meaning of existence was to preserve untarnished,
undisturbed and undistorted the image of eternity which
each person is born with—as far as possible.
Like a silver moon in a calm, still pond.[1]

n "One Word of Truth," his Nobel lecture, Solzhenitsyn mentions only four other writers: Dostoevsky (several times), Vladimir Solovyov, Albert Camus, and Heinrich Böll. The reference to Camus comes in a discussion of the social responsibilities of the artist, that to Böll in alluding to "the international brotherhood of writers." Camus and Böll had both mounted critiques of totalitarianism[2] and each had been honored with the Nobel Prize for Literature, making Solzhenitsyn's remarks all the more apposite. His affinities with Dostoevsky and Solovyov ran deeper. Solovyov (1853–1900) was a friend and confidant of Dostoevsky, and shared with his compatriots a Slavophilic understanding of Eastern Christianity, arguing that "if the faith communicated by the Church to Christian humanity is a living faith, and if the grace of the sacraments is an effectual grace, the resultant union of the divine and the human cannot be limited to the special domain of religion, but must extend to all Man's common relationships and must regenerate and transform his social and political life."[3] He was, it seems, one of the inspirations for the character of Aloysha Karamazov. Solovyov and his contemporary Nikolai Berdayev form a philosophical bridge, as it were, between Dostoevsky and Solzhenitsyn.

We opened the present volume with a discussion of Dostoevsky, arguably the greatest of all novelists; we come full circle to finish with another writer of the same homeland, perhaps the greatest of the twentieth century (can he fend off Thomas Mann?). There are many Dostoevskian reverberations in the life, thought, and art of Solzhenitsyn. Here are the bare bones of his outer life. Born during the death throes of the Great War, studied mathematics at the University of Rostov and literature at Moscow State University, fought on the Prussian front as an artillery captain and was twice decorated, arrested in 1945 for writing a letter critical of Stalin, spent eight years in prison camps and three more in exile before his rehabilitation in 1956. Began serious literary writing while working in central Russia as a maths teacher. During the short-lived de-Stalinizing "thaw" of the early '60s he published *One Day in the Life of Ivan Denisovich* (1962), often acclaimed in that self-contradictory phrase, "an instant classic," a runaway best-seller in both Russia and the West. Within a year Solzhenitsyn had fallen foul of the party apparatchiks, and was now forced to publish his writings in the underground *samizdat*. Over the next decade he produced his major works, *Cancer Ward* (1968), *The First Circle* (1968), *August 1914* (1971), and the epochal *The Gulag Archipelago* (1973–1978). He was arrested and charged with treason in 1974 and exiled from the Soviet Union. He lived for a while in Heinrich Böll's home in West Germany, then in Switzerland, and spent the rest of his exile in the United States, eventually settling in Vermont. For a while he was lauded as the anti-Communist poster-boy of the moment, but his excoriating critique of decadent Western materialism and his affirmation of traditional Orthodoxy soon saw him consigned him to the fringes. Solzhenitsyn's Soviet citizenship was restored in 1990. He and his wife returned to Russia in 1994. He died in 2008, aged eighty-nine.

Neither Dostoevsky nor Solzhenitsyn committed any real political crime; both were arrested in their late twenties by stupidly repressive regimes, subjected to brutal incarceration and to years of exile. Humiliated, punished, banished, robbed of a decade in which they might have been enjoying the fruits of a "normal" life. Each experienced a profound religious conversion in the prison camps; both had come from devout Orthodox families but had flirted with the fashionable atheistic and materialist philosophies of the West, thinking that the "ancient trinity of Truth, Goodness, and Beauty" was perhaps "an empty, faded formula";[4] their imprisonment proved to be the crucible in which a new and deeper Christian faith was forged and in which they identified more closely with "the insulted and injured." Solzhenitsyn:

> Bless you prison, bless you for being in my life. For there, lying upon the rotting prison straw, I came to realize that the object of life is not prosperity as we are made to believe, but the maturity of the human soul.[5]

Each drew on these experiences to produce graphic literary works: *House of the Dead* and *One Day in the Life of Ivan Denisovich*. Both went on to write novels that stand as towering landmarks in world literature, works in which the problem of evil and the nature of human destiny are explored with frightening insight and deep compassion. In neither case did their appalling treatment by authoritarian regimes drive them, as might have been expected, into Western democratic liberalism, seen by both as, at best, a superficial and anodyne political ideology—"liberals are men made of paper," said Dostoevsky[6]—and at worst as a symptom of the profound spiritual malaise of the West. Each produced a scorching indictment of the progressivist and revolutionary ideologies of their time, most devastatingly in *The Possessed* and *The Gulag Archipelago*. Both decisively repudiated the false gospel of "Progress." Solzhenitsyn: "All the glorified technological achievements of Progress, including the conquest of outer space, do not redeem the Twentieth century's moral poverty which no one could imagine even as late as in the Nineteenth Century."[7] (He might have added that there was one man who did imagine the "moral poverty of the twentieth-century man"; Dostoevsky.) Both came to favor what could most charitably be described as benignly authoritarian forms of government.[8] Each diagnosed the "death of God" as the root cause of the barbarism and bestiality of the modern era. Their spiritual brotherhood, if one might put it that way, stemmed from their faith in Christ and His teachings, and in the universal mission of the Orthodox Church. Both writers took on a prophetic role in their vision of the destiny not only of Russia but of the whole of humankind. No doubt one could tease out many other arresting parallels. One might, for example, draw attention to the fact that each had an astonishingly creative mid-life surge. Dostoevsky's golden run extended from *Notes from Underground* in 1864, through *Crime and Punishment*, *The Idiot*, and *The Possessed*, to *The Brothers Karamazov* in 1880. Solzhenitsyn produced all his major works between 1962 and 1978. A sixteen-year streak in each case, Dostoevsky's launched when he was 43, Solzhenitsyn's when he was 44. Both believed in the creative and redemptive power of art and of the "one word of truth" that "outweighs the world."

In Solzhenitsyn's Templeton Address of 1983 we find this oft-quoted passage:

> More than half a century ago, while I was still a child, I recall hearing a number of older people offer the following explanation for

the great disasters that had befallen Russia: "Men have forgotten God; that's why all this has happened." Since then I have spent well-nigh fifty years working on the history of our Revolution; in the process I have read hundreds of books, collected hundreds of personal testimonies, and have already contributed eight volumes of my own toward the effort of clearing away the rubble left by that upheaval. But if I were asked today to formulate as concisely as possible the main cause of the ruinous Revolution that swallowed up some sixty million of our people, I could not put it more accurately than to repeat: "Men have forgotten God; that's why all this has happened."

The passage echoes Ivan Karamazov's ominous portent "If God doesn't exist, everything is permitted." Nietzsche's dire declaration becomes the herald of a new age of barbarism, inspired by the atheistic and progressivist ideologies of the day. Both novelists link the collapse of religious faith to the intoxicating promise of untrammelled "freedom." Here is Solzhenitsyn in sombre mood, pondering the American development of the same disease that Dostoevsky embodied in Raskolnikov, Peter Verkhovensky, Kirillov, all the delirious revolutionary Utopians of his time:

> in early democracies, as in American democracy at the time of its birth, all individual human rights were granted on the ground that man is God's creature. That is, freedom was given to the individual conditionally, in the assumption of his constant religious responsibility. Such was the heritage of the preceding one thousand years. Two hundred or even fifty years ago, it would have seemed quite impossible, in America, that an individual be granted boundless freedom with no purpose, simply for the satisfaction of his whims. Subsequently, however, all such limitations were eroded everywhere in the West; a total emancipation occurred from the moral heritage of Christian centuries with their great reserves of mercy and sacrifice. State systems were becoming ever more materialistic. The West has finally achieved the rights of man, and even to excess, but man's sense of responsibility to God and society has grown dimmer and dimmer.[9]

Elsewhere Solzhenitsyn is at pains to stress that atheism is the motive force of Communist ideology, manifest in the totalitarian state's relentless persecution of the Church. In doing so he acknowl-

edges his debt to Dostoevsky, whom he described as "a man of fan-
tastic illumination":

> It was Dostoevsky, once again, who drew from the French Revolu-
> tion and its seeming hatred of the Church the lesson that "revolu-
> tion must necessarily begin with atheism." That is absolutely true.
> But the world had never before known a godlessness as organized,
> militarized, and tenaciously malevolent as that practiced by Marx-
> ism. Within the philosophical system of Marx and Lenin, and at
> the heart of their psychology, hatred of God is the principal driv-
> ing force, more fundamental than all their political and economic
> pretensions. Militant atheism is not merely incidental or marginal
> to Communist policy; it is not a side effect, but the central pivot.[10]

As Lenin himself had declared "Atheism is the natural and inseparable part of Communism." What both Dostoevsky and Solzhenitsyn
foresaw with such chilling acuity was the inevitable substitution of a
new Absolute, a new Deity which was nothing other than naked
Power, whose avatars were Marxism-Leninism (the new scripture),
the Party, the State, the Leader, all to be used to justify unimaginable
horrors and suffering beyond measure. In his exposure of the Gulag
Archipelago and all its sinister apparatus, in confronting this evil
head-on, Solzhenitsyn displayed the most extraordinary courage
and moral heroism. *Ivan Denisovich*, *Cancer Ward*, *The First Circle*,
and *The Gulag Archipelago* put Solzhenitsyn in the very front rank of
novelists who have plumbed the nightmarish depths of godless ideologies and totalitarian regimes—Dostoevsky, Kafka, Orwell, Koes-
tler, Zamyatin, Huxley.

The loss of religious faith produced a different monster in the
West, the worship of Mammon:

> On the way from the Renaissance to our days we have enriched
> our experience, but we have lost the concept of a Supreme Com-
> plete Entity [i.e., God] which used to restrain our passions and
> our irresponsibility. We have placed too much hope in political
> and social reforms, only to find out that we were being deprived of
> our most precious possession: our spiritual life. In the East, it is
> destroyed by the dealings and machinations of the ruling party. In
> the West, commercial interests tend to suffocate it. This is the real
> crisis.[11]

Religion is replaced by ideology, *always* with results fatal to humankind's spiritual welfare, regardless of the ideology in question. Fascism and Communism—ideology in its most evil guises—opened the Gates of Hell in Auschwitz and Siberia. But *all* profane ideologies, unharnessed from religious values, create spiritual wastelands.

> Ideology—that is what gives evildoing its long-sought justifications and gives the evildoer the necessary steadfastness and determination. That is the social theory which helps to make his acts seem good instead of bad in his own and others' eyes, so that he won't hear reproaches and curses but will receive praise and honors. That was how the agents of the Inquisition fortified their wills: by invoking Christianity; the conquerors of foreign lands, by extolling the grandeur of their Motherland; the colonizers, by civilization; the Nazis, by race; and the Jacobins (early and late), by equality, brotherhood, and the happiness of future generations. . . . Thanks to ideology the twentieth century was fated to experience evildoing calculated on a scale in the millions.[12]

We might recall Trotsky's response when asked what he thought of the fact that the Russian Civil War had cost some 6 million lives, "A small price to pay for the Revolution."

Any properly constituted political philosophy must, in Solzhenitsyn's view, evolve within a religious framework and pay due attention to our spiritual as well as material welfare—a proposition that sticks in the craw of modern ideologues of all stripes. Of course, there is another danger lurking in the fusion of politics and "religion" of a belligerent, fundamentalist, and exclusivist kind, as history testifies. No shortage of examples in the modern world either. But that unhappy subject is beyond our present scope.

Here, in *The Gulag Archipelago*, is Solzhenitsyn on the Communist State's systematic and ruthless campaign in the '20s and '30s to destroy Orthodoxy root and branch, a campaign more or less completely ignored by the progressivist "intelligentsia" of the West. It is worth quoting at some length.

> The root destruction of religion in the country, which throughout the twenties and thirties was one of the most important goals of the GPU-NKVD, could be realized only by mass arrests of Ortho-

dox believers. Monks and nuns, whose black habits had been a distinctive feature of Old Russian life, were intensively rounded up on every hand, placed under arrest, and sent into exile. They arrested and sentenced active laymen. The circles kept getting bigger, as they raked in ordinary believers as well, old people and particularly women, who were the most stubborn believers of all and who, for many long years to come, would be called "nuns" in transit prisons and in camps. . . . In the twenties the religious education of children was classified as a political crime under Article 58-10 of the Code—in other words, counterrevolutionary propaganda! . . . All persons convicted of religious activity received "tenners," the longest term then given.

Solzhenitsyn found grounds for hope in the tenacious survival of Russian Orthodoxy: "It is here that we see the dawn of hope: for no matter how formidably Communism bristles with tanks and rockets, no matter what successes it attains in seizing the planet, it is doomed never to vanquish Christianity."[13]

As a Christian, Solzhenitsyn did not claim that evil originated in either ideologies or in political institutions: evil originated in the human heart. Evil was a datum of human experience. As the Christian tradition teaches, we are fallen creatures, living in an imperfect world, all capable of great evil. As Dostoevsky had written in *House of the Dead*, "It's hard to imagine to what an extent a man's nature can be corrupted." In a famous passage in *The Gulag Archipelago* Solzhenitsyn writes,

> Gradually it was disclosed to me that the line separating good and evil passes not through states, nor between classes, nor between political parties either—but right through every human heart— and through all human hearts. This line shifts. Inside us, it oscillates with the years. And even within hearts overwhelmed by evil, one small bridgehead of good is retained. And even in the best of all hearts, there remains an unuprooted small corner of evil. Since then I have come to understand the truth of all the religions of the world: They struggle with the evil inside a human being (inside every human being). It is impossible to expel evil from the world in its entirety, but it is possible to constrict it within each person.

"Human rights" and other such secular-political values are not to be dismissed, but they are no bulwark against evil. "A society with unlimited rights is incapable of standing to adversity. If we do not wish to be ruled by a coercive authority, then each of us must rein himself in. . . . A stable society is achieved not by balancing opposing forces but by conscious self-limitation. . . ."[14]

But at the same time as we harbor within us the capacity for evil we are made in God's image; there is a Divine Spark at the heart of our being. As a character in *Cancer Ward* says, "Sometimes I feel quite distinctly that what is inside me is not all of me. There is something else, sublime, quite indestructible, some tiny fragment of the Universal spirit. Don't you feel that?"[15] Elsewhere Solzhenitsyn speaks of the way in which the Creator participates in our daily existence:

> Our life consists not in the pursuit of material success but in the quest for worthy spiritual growth. Our entire earthly existence is but a transitional stage in the movement toward something higher, and we must not stumble and fall, nor must we linger fruitlessly on one rung of the ladder. Material laws alone do not explain our life or give it direction. The laws of physics and physiology will never reveal the indisputable manner in which the Creator constantly, day in and day out, participates in the life of each of us, unfailingly granting us the energy of existence; when this assistance leaves us, we die. And in the life of our entire planet, the Divine Spirit surely moves with no less force: this we must grasp in our dark and terrible hour.[16]

The political question is how our social organization and our governance can be constituted so as to honor our natures as spiritual beings *and* to promote our earthly welfare by encouraging the good and constraining the bad, adhering to "the principle that we are always duty-bound to defer to the sense of moral justice." Philosophically and morally, humanism does not answer the needs of the case:

> If humanism were right in declaring that man is born to be happy, he would not be born to die. Since his body is doomed to die, his task on earth evidently must be of a more spiritual nature. It cannot be the unrestrained enjoyment of everyday life. It cannot be the search for the best ways to obtain material goods and then cheerfully

get the most out of them. It has to be the fulfillment of a permanent, earnest duty so that one's life journey may become an experience of moral growth. . . . Only voluntary, inspired self-restraint can raise man above the world stream of materialism.[17]

Furthermore, "Untouched by the breath of God, unrestricted by human conscience, both capitalism and socialism are repulsive."[18]

Here we are too constrained to explore either Solzhenitsyn's political philosophy or his theology in any detail. Nor can we delve further into his temperament and sensibility—but here are a few random pointers:

Human nature, if it changes at all, changes not much faster than the geological face of the earth (*The Gulag Archipelago*).

Communism is as crude an attempt to explain society and the individual as if a surgeon were to perform his delicate operations with a meat ax. All that is subtle in human psychology and in the structure of society . . . is reduced to crude economic processes. The whole created being—man—is reduced to matter. It is characteristic that Communism is so devoid of arguments that it has none to advance against its opponents in our Communist countries. It lacks arguments and hence there is the club, the prison, the concentration camp, and insane asylums with forced confinement (Warning to the West).[19]

Nothing is more boring than a man with a career (*The Gulag Archipelago*).

To stand up for truth is nothing. For truth, you must sit in jail (*The Gulag Archipelago*).

Hastiness and superficiality are the psychic diseases of the twentieth century (*A World Split Apart*).

A great writer is, so to speak, a second government in his country. And for that reason no regime has ever loved great writers, only minor ones (*The First Circle*).

Pride grows in the human heart like lard on a pig (*The Gulag Archipelago*).

Without any censorship, in the West fashionable trends of thought and ideas are carefully separated from those which are not fashionable; nothing is forbidden, but what is not fashionable will hardly ever find its way into periodicals or books or be heard in colleges (*A World Split Apart*).

The solemn pledge to abstain from telling the truth was called socialist realism (*One Word of Truth*).

This eager fanning of the flames of hatred is becoming the mark of today's free world. Indeed, the broader the personal freedoms are, the higher the level of prosperity or even of abundance—the more vehement, paradoxically, does this blind hatred become (*Men have forgotten God*).

That which is called humanism, but what would be more correctly called irreligious anthropocentrism, cannot yield answers to the most essential questions of our life (Joseph Pearce interview).

The Western world has lost its civil courage, both as a whole and separately, in each country, each government, each political party and of course in the United Nations. Such a decline in courage is particularly noticeable among the ruling groups and the intellectual elite… (*A World Split Apart*).

If private enterprise isn't held in an iron grip it gives birth to people who are no better than beasts, those stock-exchange people with greedy appetites beyond restraint (*Cancer Ward*).

I leaf through the ancient philosophers and find my newest discoveries there (*A World Split Apart*).

God is endlessly multi-dimensional, so every religion that exists on earth represents some face, some side of God (Joseph Pearce interview).

On the occasion of Solzhenitsyn's death my friend Brian Coman penned an essay that he concluded with some lines from a prayer the novelist composed after he was catapulted to fame. I hope Brian will not mind if I follow his example.

Atop the ridge of earthly fame,
I look back in wonder at the path which I alone could never
Have found,
A wondrous path through despair to this point
From which I too, could transmit to mankind
A reflection of Your Rays.

And as much as I must still reflect
You will give me.
But as much as I cannot take up
You will have already assigned to others.[20]

Endnotes

FYODOR MIKHAILOVICH DOSTOEVSKY

1 Dostoevsky quoted in Victor Frankl, *Man's Search for Meaning*; *www.a wakin.org/read/view.php?tid=*601.

2 If you want to know everything that can be known about Dostoevsky's life, go to Joseph Frank's five-volume, *Dostoevsky: A Writer in His Time*, 2002; but most readers would settle for the single-volume condensed version published in 2010. For more modest biographies see: E. H. Carr, *Dostoevsky 1821–1881*, 1962; David Magarshack, *Dostoevsky*, 1963; Geir Kjetsaa, *Dostoevsky, A Writer's Life*, 1988.

3 Helpful secondary sources on Dostoevsky's religious thought include Nicholas Berdayev, *Dostoevsky*, 1957; Alexander Boyce Gibson, *The Religion of Dostoevsky*, 1974; Eduard Thurneysen, *Dostoevsky: A Theological Study*, 1964. An important recent addition to this literature is Rowan Williams' *Dostoevsky: Language, Faith, and Fiction*, 2008.

4 Among these prejudices were anti-Semitism, an animus to Roman Catholicism and Protestantism, and a sometimes globally xenophobic attitude to the "decadent" West. Dostoevsky's worst characteristics—of which he was well aware and against which he struggled—are on particularly unattractive display in his crude and brutal outbursts about Turks during and after the Russo-Turkish War of 1877.

5 Joseph Frank, Dostoevsky: *A Writer in His Time*, 2010, 579.

6 From a letter to his niece, quoted in Geir Kjetsaa, *Fyodor Dostoevsky*, 1987, 221–22. One of the more successful attempts to create an "absolutely good" character was Willa Cather's in *My Antonia* (1918).

7 E. H. Carr, *Dostoevsky*, 163.

8 https://www.artstor.org/2019/07/17/dostoevsky-and-the-challenge-of-hans-holbeins-dead-christ/.

9 Nicholas Berdayev, *Dostoevsky*, 31.

10 *The Idiot*, David McDuff translation, Penguin Classics, 2004.

11 These observations come from Dostoevsky's friend Baron Alexander Ergovich Wrangel; Wikipedia entry on Dostoevsky.

12 Metropolitan Anthony of Sourozh, *God and Man*, 1974, 68.

13 *The Gay Science*, 1882; taken from *The Vision of Nietzsche*, ed. Philip Novak, 1996, 58.

14 Kaufmann cited at: academyofideas.com/2012/11/nietzsche-and-the-death-of-god/.
15 Nietzsche cited in Ernest Heller, *The Importance of Nietzsche*, 1988, 5.
16 Nietzsche, *The Will to Power*, Heller's translation.
17 Dostoevsky's notes for *The Idiot*, cited in Geir Kjetsaa, 224.
18 George Steiner, *Tolstoy or Dostoevsky*, 1967, 307.
19 From *The Brothers Karamazov*. Concerning the controversy about the translation of the passage in question, see Andrei I. Volkov, "Dostoevsky Did Say It: A Response to David E. Cortesi"; https://infidels.org/library/modern/andrei_volkov/dostoevsky.html.
20 Nicholas Berdayev, *Dostoevsky*, 22.

RUDOLF OTTO

1   Rudolf Otto, *The Idea of the Holy*, 1958, 5.
2   This is a severely edited and revised version of an essay which appeared in *Religion and Retributive Logic: Essays in Honour of Professor Garry W. Trompf*, ed. Carole M. Cusack and Christopher Hartney, Leiden: Brill, 2010; 229–44.
3   Otto never wrote about his own life in any detail but did compose an autobiographical sketch in 1891, recently translated and published as "My Life" in *Autobiographical and Social Essays*, ed. G. D. Alles, 1996, 50–61. A short biographical sketch of Otto can be found in H. Turner & P. Mackenzie, *Commentary on "The Idea of the Holy,"* Aberdeen, no date.
4   R. Otto, "My Life," 51–52.
5   Barth quoted in *Autobiographical and Social Essays*, 9.
6   See P. Almond, Rudolf Otto: *An Introduction to His Philosophical Theology*, 1984, 24–25.
7   See J. Harvey, Translator's Preface, *The Idea of the Holy*, 1958, xix.
8   N. Söderblom, "Holiness" in J. Hastings (ed), *Encyclopedia of Religion and Ethics*, Vol. 6, 1913.
9   R. Otto, *The Idea of the Holy*, 7.
10 Ibid., 17.
11 In Turner & Mackenzie, *Commentary on "The Idea of the Holy,"* 4.
12 Benz quoted in *Autobiographical and Social Essays*, 61.
13 Quoted in P. Almond, *Rudolf Otto*, 23–24. For a similar epiphany experienced by a Western Christian in the face of traditional sculptures see Thomas Merton's account of his encounter with the Buddha figures of Polanuwurra (Sri Lanka) in N. Burton et al. (eds), *The*

Asian Journal of Thomas Merton, 1972, 33–36; the passage is cited in the essay on Merton in the present volume. Fr Henri Le Saux (Swami Abhishiktananda) was "thunderstruck" by his encounter with the great figure of Siva Maheswara at Elephanta, describing it as "one of those high points that light up one's life"; see Abhishiktananda, *Ascent to the Depth of the Heart*, Delhi, 1998, 105–6. Fr Bede Griffiths' account of a very similar experience at Elephanta can be found in *The Marriage of East and West*, 1982, 10–11.

14 R. Otto, *Mysticism East and West: A Comparative Analysis of the Nature of Mysticism*, 1957, v.

15 *The Idea of the Holy*, 21.

16 See H. Rollmann, "Rudolf Otto and India," *Religious Studies Review*, 5:3, July 1979, 199–203. Rollman provides a full bibliography of Otto's Indological writings, some 70-odd in all.

17 J. Wach, *Types of Religious Experience*, 216.

18 R. Otto, *Autobiographical and Social Essays*, 195–96.

19 Ibid., 203.

20 See P. Almond, "Rudolf Otto and Buddhism," in Masefield & Wiebe (eds), *Aspects of Religion: Essays in Honor of Ninian Smart*, 1994, 60.

21 "Buddhism, Islam and the irrational" (1932), in *Autobiographical and Social Essays*, 190–91.

22 E. M. Cioran, *Anathemas and Admirations* (1947), tr. Richard Howard, 1991, 188.

23 R. Otto, *Autobiographical and Social Essays*, 145.

24 "A League of Nations is not enough," Ibid., 146.

25 S. H. Nasr, *Sufi Essays*, 1972, 127.

26 R. Otto quoted in P. Almond, "Rudolf Otto and Buddhism," 69.

27 "A League of Nations is not enough," 148.

28 G. Alles in R. Otto, *Autobiographical and Social Essays*, 11.

EVELYN UNDERHILL

1 Evelyn Underhill, *Mysticism*, 2002, 24.

2 There are two full-dress biographies: Christopher J. R. Armstrong, *Evelyn Underhill (1875–1941): An Introduction to her Life and Works*, 1975; and Dana Greene, *Evelyn Underhill: Artist of the Infinite Life*, 1991.

3 Wikipedia, "Evelyn Underhill."

4 Joy Milos, "Underhill's Mysticism: A Centenary Review," http://evelynunderhill.org/.

5 http://evelynunderhill.org/about/.

6 Wikipedia.

7 Joy Milos, "Underhill's Mysticism: A Centenary Review."

8 https://www.azquotes.com/quote/1139593.

9 I Corinthians 2:11. As Thomas Merton tersely puts it, "God cannot be understood except by Himself"; *New Seeds of Contemplation.*

10 Evelyn Underhill, *Practical Mysticism*, 2014, 10.

11 Anne Bancroft, *Weavers of Wisdom: Women Mystics of the Twentieth Century*, 1989, 92.

12 The nature of this mystical annihilation is discussed more fully elsewhere in this volume, in the essay on Abhishiktananda.

13 https://www.azquotes.com/quote/1015208.

14 Underhill, *Mysticism*, 79.

15 Frithjof Schuon, *Survey of Metaphysics and Esoterism*, 1986, 165.

16 Frithjof Schuon, *Logic and Transcendence*, 1975, 204 n9.

17 Martin Lings, *What is Sufism?*, 1975, 93.

18 *The Unanimous Tradition: Essays on the Essential Unity of All Religions*, ed. Ranjit Fernando, 1991, 89–95.

19 https://ccel.org/ccel/underhill/mysticism/mysticism.i_1.html.

20 Foreword to Christopher J. R. Armstrong, *Evelyn Underhill*, 1975, x.

21 https://www.sacred-texts.com/myst/myst/myst01.htm.

22 Evelyn Underhill, *The Golden Sequence* (1933), quoted in Bancroft, *Weavers of Wisdom*, 93.

A.P. ELKIN

1 A.P. Elkin, *Aboriginal Men of High Degree*, 1977, 171.

2 The only detailed (and over-critical) biography is by Tigger Wise, *The Self-Made Anthropologist: A Life of A.P. Elkin*, 1985. A short biographical sketch by the same author can be found in the *Australian Dictionary of Biography*.

3 "Tuckiar" was the European appellation, later changed to "Takiara." More recently he is referred to as "Dhakiyarr Wirrrpanda." Australian film-maker Tom Murray's Dhakiyarr vs. the King (2005) recounts the story and portrays the efforts of his descendants to restore his honor.

4 "Introduction" to W.E. Harney, *Taboo*, 1949, 6.

5 The second limb of the title was dropped in later editions.

6 Tigger Wise, "Elkin, Adolphus Peter (1891–1979)," *Australian Dictionary of Biography*.

7 See Martin Thomas & Margo Neale (eds), *Exploring the Legacy of the*

1948 Arnhem Land Expedition, 2011, 8–10. C. P. Mountford (1890–1976) was a photographer, explorer and an "amateur" anthropologist with a special interest in Aboriginal art. He led several anthropological expeditions in central and northern Australia.

8 Jonathan Lane, "Anchorage in Aboriginal affairs: A. P. Elkin on religious continuity and civic obligation," University of Sydney PhD thesis, 2007; 312. (The thesis is available at https:/ses.library.usyd.edu.au/handle/2123/3691?show=full).

9 W. E. H. Stanner, "Religion, Totemism and Symbolism" (1965) in *Religion in Aboriginal Australia*, ed. Max Charlesworth et al., 1984, 155.

10 See *Aboriginal Men of High Degree*, 57–64.

11 On Harney see Jennifer J. Kennedy's entry in the *Australian Dictionary of Biography*.

12 William Paden, *Religious Worlds*, 1988, 51.

13 Jonathan Lane, 361.

14 Tigger Wise, *The Self-Made Anthropologist*, 248.

DOROTHY SAYERS

1 *The Letters of Dorothy L. Sayers Vol II: 1937–1943*, 2014, 43.

2 This, obviously, was before Lewis's marriage, at the age of fifty-seven, to the American writer, Joy Davidman.

3 Preface to Chesterton's play, *The Surprise*, 1952.

4 From the chapter "Free Will and Miracle" in *The Making of Man*.

5 The Lewis review appeared in *Theology*, 1941.

6 www.wheaton.edu/academics/academic-centers/wadecenter/authors/dorothy-l-sayers/.

7 Sayers, *Creed or Chaos?*

8 Sayers, *Letters to a Diminished Church*.

9 Sayers, Ibid.

10 Sayers, *Introductory Dante Papers*.

11 These quotations come from *Whose Body*, *Gaudy Night*, *The Nine Tailors*, and *Clouds of Witness*.

12 This excerpt and those following about the nature of work come from a 1942 address entitled "Why Work?" later appearing in *Creed or Chaos?* A slightly edited version of *Why Work?* can be found in *The Betrayal of Tradition*, ed. Harry Oldmeadow, 2005. It is also available on the web at: https://www1.villanova.edu/.

13 See Roger Sworder, *Mining, Metallurgy and the Meaning of Life*, 1995, esp., Ch 6.
14 The publication is *Are Women Human?*, the title coming from an address Sayers gave in 1938.

BEDE GRIFFITHS

1 Bede Griffiths, *The Marriage of East and West*, 1982, 24–25.
2 Biographical material taken primarily from Bede Griffiths, *The Golden String*, 1964, and Wayne Teasdale, "Bede Griffiths as a Visionary Guide," the Introduction to *The Other Half of My Soul*, ed. Beatrice Bruteau, 1996. The fullest biography of Griffiths is by Shirley du Boulay, *Beyond the Darkness: A Biography of Bede Griffiths*, 1998; there is also a good deal of biographical material in Judson Trapnell's *Bede Griffiths: A Life in Dialogue*, 2001. An earlier biography by Katherine Spink, *A Sense of the Sacred: A Biography of Bede Griffiths*, 1988, is a comparatively flimsy affair.
3 Bede Griffiths, *The Golden String*, 9.
4 Ibid., 13–14.
5 Helen Luke, "Bede Griffiths at Apple Farm" in *The Other Half of My Soul*, 39.
6 Wayne Teasdale, "Bede Griffiths as a Visionary Guide," 7.
7 Recounted in Shirley du Boulay, *Beyond the Darkness*.
8 Matthew Fox & Bede Griffiths, "Spirituality for a New Era," in *The Other Half of My Soul*, 315. Compare Griffiths' remark with Karl Rahner: "The Christian of the future will be a mystic or he or she will not exist at all," from *The Practice of Faith* (1985), quoted in *Beyond the Darkness*, 269.
9 M. Fox, *Confessions: The Makings of a Postdenominational Priest*, 1996, 214.
10 Bede Griffiths, Diary, quoted in *Beyond the Darkness*, 328.
11 L. Freeman, "Bede Griffiths," *Vedanta for East and West*, 254, Nov–Dec 1993, 282.
12 This trajectory has been traced by Joel Smith in "Religious Diversity, Hindu-Christian Dialogue and Bede Griffiths," in *Proceedings of the Eighth International Symposium on Asian Studies*, Hong Kong: Asian Research Studies, 1986.
13 Bede Griffiths, "Symbolism and Cult" (1956), quoted in *Beyond the Darkness*, 117 (italics mine).
14 It is highly unlikely that Griffiths had actually read Guénon at this

point, though he certainly did later in life. He also read the works of several other traditionalists and acclaimed Seyyed Hossein Nasr's *Knowledge and the Sacred* as the most authoritative exposition of the perennial philosophy he had encountered. See *Beyond the Darkness*, 197.

15 *The Marriage of East and West*, 1982, 24–25.

16 Ibid., 42–43.

17 See J.B. Trapnell, "Bede Griffiths, Mystical Knowing, and the Unity of Religions," in *Philosophy and Theology*, 7:4, Summer, 1993.

18 Frithjof Schuon, "No Activity Without Truth," *The Sword of Gnosis*, ed. J. Needleman, 1974, 29.

19 See also Schuon's *Stations of Wisdom*, 1961, 11.

20 See Rama P. Coomaraswamy, "The Desacralisation of Hinduism for Western Consumption," *Sophia*, 4:2, Winter 1998, esp. 203.

SIMONE WEIL

1 Simone Weil, *Waiting for God*, 1973, 175.

2 Heather Macrobie, "Should we still read Simone Weil?" *The Guardian*, February 4, 2009.

3 Clive James, another polymath apparently determined to proffer opinions about almost every important cultural/intellectual figure of the twentieth century, wisely steers clear of Weil. His 900-page compendium of modern thinkers, *Cultural Amnesia* (2007) makes not a single mention of her. Perhaps a case of discretion being the better part…

4 James Cowan, "Simone Weil's Journey through Fire," in *A Spanner in the Works*, 2008, 90.

5 The most detailed account of her life is to be found in the biography by her friend Simone Pétrement, *Simone Weil: A Life*, 1976. A shorter biography is *Simone Weil* by Francine Du Plessix-Gray, 2001. The most important autobiographical essay is "Letter IV: Spiritual Autobiography" in *Waiting for God*, 61–83. A useful overview of both her life and work can be found in the Wikipedia entry "Simone Weil."

6 Rowan Williams, *Luminaries: Twenty lives that illuminate the Christian Way*, 2019, 125.

7 *Waiting for God*, 68–69.

8 Ibid., 69.

9 Richard Rees, *Simone Weil: A Sketch for a Portrait*, 1966, 191; quoted in Wikipedia. See also James Cowan, "Simone Weil's Journey through Fire," 87–102.

10 Susan Sontag, "Simone Weil" from *Against Interpretation*, in *The Susan Sontag Reader*, ed. Elizabeth Hardwick, 1982, 92.

11 From Leslie Fiedler's Introduction to the 1973 edition of *Waiting on God*, 31.

12 These have been taken from my notebook where, over the years, I have copied such things without documenting their provenance. Most of them come from *Waiting on God* and *Gravity and Grace* and are easily tracked down on the internet, as are many of the other short quotes in this essay.

13 Weil quoted in Christy Wampole, "Strange and Intelligent"; https://aeon.co/essays.

14 From *The Need for Roots*, in Christy Wampole.

15 *On the Abolition of All Political Parties*, quoted by Maria Popova, brainpickings.org/2018/10/31.

16 *Waiting for God*, 159–60 (italics mine).

17 "Human Personality"; lib.tcu.edu/staff/bellinger/rel-viol/Weil.pdf. See also a lucid exposition of Weil's complex ideas about justice, somewhat over-simplified in the present discussion, in Ann Tyndall, "Gravity and Grace: Justice in the Thought of Simone Weil," in *The Last Platonist*, ed. Maurice Nestor and Brian Coman, 2017, 241.

18 *Gravity and Grace*, 2002, 117.

19 *Waiting for God*, 182. In her *Notebooks* Weil wrote this: "The primitive Zen method seems to consist of a gratuitous search of such intensity that it takes the place of all attachments. But, because it is gratuitous, it cannot become an object of attachment except in so far as it is actively pursued, and the activity involved in this fruitless search is exhausted. When exhaustion point has been almost reached, some shock or other brings about detachment. . . . The idea behind Zen Buddhism is to perceive purely, without any admixture of reverie. . . ."; quoted in Iris Murdoch, *Metaphysics as a Guide to Morals*, 1993, 247. For more information on Weil's Eastern engagements see: simoneweilbibliography.blogspot.com/2014/02/simone-and-buddhism, and Elisa Aaltola, "Confronting suffering with narrative theory, constructed selfhood, and control: Critical perspectives by Simone Weil and Buddhist metaphysics," *Journal of Disability and Religion*, 23:3, 2019.

20 Mark Stone, "Dweller on the Threshold: Simone Weil and Perennialism," *Crossing Religious Frontiers*, ed. Harry Oldmeadow, in the *Studies in Comparative Religion* series, 2010, 145.

21 This is a condensation of several passages from *Waiting for God* in

Anne Bancroft, *Weavers of Wisdom: Women Mystics of the Twentieth Century*, 1989, 95.

22 *Waiting for God*, 77.

23 Ibid., 185.

24 Rowan Williams, *Luminaries*, 129.

25 George Steiner, "Sainte Simone—Simone Weil," in *No Passion Spent: Essays 1978–1996*, 1996, 177.

26 For a cogent refutation of parts of Steiner's critique see Mark Stone, "Dweller on the Threshold."

27 George Steiner, "Sainte Simone—Simone Weil," 179.

28 *Gravity and Grace*, 5.

29 Weil quoted in Mark Stone, "Dweller on the Threshold," 147.

ABHISHIKTANANDA

1 Taken from *Mediations: Essays on Religious Pluralism and the Perennial Philosophy*, 2008, and largely comprising excerpts from *A Christian Pilgrim in India: The Spiritual Journey of Swami Abhishiktananda*, 2008. Many issues which are only touched on here are explored in more depth in the book.

2 From Abhishiktananda, "Le Père Monchanin," in A. Rawlinson, *Book of Enlightened Masters*, 1997, 148.

3 Most of the biographical material which follows is taken from J.G. Weber, *In Quest of the Absolute: the Life and Work of Jules Monchanin*, 1977.

4 Ibid., 72–73.

5 Ibid., 21–22.

6 E. Vattakuzhy, *Indian Christian Sannyasa and Swami Abhishiktananda*, 1981, 67.

7 Weber, *In Quest of the Absolute*, 16.

8 Ibid., 97.

9 Ibid., 25.

10 Ibid., 77–78, 82, 126.

11 S.H. Nasr, *Sufi Essays*, 1972, 127.

12 O. Baumer-Despeigne, "The Spiritual Journey of Henri Le Saux-Abhishiktananda," *Cistercian Studies*, 1983, 313.

13 F. Schuon, *Language of the Self*, 1959, 44.

14 J.M.D. Stuart, "Sri Ramana Maharshi and Abhishiktananda," *Vidjajyoti*, April, 1980, 170.

15 O. Baumer-Despeigne, "The Spiritual Journey," 316.

16 J. E. Royster, "Abhishiktananda: Hindu-Christian Monk," *Studies in Formative Spirituality* 9:3, 1988, 311.

17 Abhishiktananda, *Guru and Disciple*, 1974, 162.

18 O. Baumer-Despeigne, "The Spiritual Journey," 327–28.

19 Abhishiktananda, *The Further Shore*, 1975, 27.

20 O. Baumer-Despeigne, "The Spiritual Journey," 327.

21 J. M. D. Stuart, "Sri Ramana Maharshi and Abhishiktananda," 173.

22 F. Schuon, *Stations of Wisdom*, 16.

23 O. Baumer-Despeigne, "The Spiritual Journey," 320.

24 F. Schuon, *Logic and Transcendence*, 144.

25 F. Schuon, *The Transfiguration of Man*, 1995, 8.

26 Abhishiktananda, *Guru and Disciple*, xi.

27 Abhishiktananda, *Saccidananda: A Christian Experience of Advaita*, 1984, 172.

28 Ibid., xiii.

29 Wayne Teasdale, "Bede Griffiths as a Visionary Guide," in *The Other Half of My Soul: Bede Griffiths and the Hindu-Christian Dialogue*, ed. Beatrice Bruteau, 1994, 14.

30 J. E. Royster, "Abhishiktananda: Hindu-Christian Monk," 308.

31 Abhishiktananda, *The Further Shore*, 42–43.

THOMAS MERTON

1 Thomas Merton, *The Silent Life*, 1957, 172.

2 In England it appeared, after editing by Evelyn Waugh, as *Elected Silence*.

3 Biographical material taken primarily from Thomas Merton, *The Seven Storey Mountain*, 1976, and Monica Furlong, *Merton: A Biography*, 1980.

4 T. Merton, *The Seven Storey Mountain*, 111.

5 Ibid., 225.

6 Ibid., 316.

7 Some, such as Matthew Fox, have speculated on the possibility that Merton was actually assassinated by the CIA. See M. Fox, *Confessions: The Making of a Post-Denominational Priest*, 1996, 73–74.

8 See M. Furlong, *Merton: A Biography*. 215.

9 See Marco Pallis, "Thomas Merton, 1915–1968," *Studies in Comparative Religion*, 3:3, 1969, 138–46.

10 T. Merton, *The Asian Journal of Thomas Merton*, 1972, 33–36.

11 See Patrick Hart, in T. Merton, *Asian Journal*, xxvii.

12 See Irmgard Schloegl's *Introduction to Thomas Merton on Zen*, 1976, vii–x.

13 I have been unable to trace this quote, which I had copied into a notebook—but it is so eloquent, and so Mertonian, that I have included it anyway.

HUSTON SMITH

1 Huston Smith, *Beyond the Postmodern Mind*.

2 Huston Smith, *Religions of Man*, 1958, 11.

3 Bede Griffiths, *The Golden String*, 1964, 13–14.

4 See *A Seat at the Table: Huston Smith in Conversation with Native Americans on Religious Freedom*, 2006.

5 For biographical details see Huston Smith's autobiography, *Tales of Wonder*, 2009; "Biographical Sketch" in Arvind Sharma (ed), *Fragments of Infinity: Essays in Philosophy and Religion, A Festschrift in Honor of Huston Smith*, 1991; M. Darrol Bryant in *Huston Smith, Essays on World Religion*, 1993; Huston Smith, *Why Religion Matters*, 2001. See also Seyyed Hossein Nasr, "Homage to Huston Smith on His Eightieth Birthday," *Sophia*, 3:2, Winter 1997.

6 Philip Novak, "The Chun-Tzu," in *Fragments of Infinity*, 8.

7 Arvind Sharma in *Fragments of Infinity*, xi–xii.

8 From *The World's Religions*.

9 Back cover of Huston Smith, *The Soul of Christianity*, 2005.

10 *The Soul of Christianity*, ix.

11 Huston Smith in H. Smith & David Ray Griffin, *Primordial Truth and Postmodern Theology*, 1989, 13.

12 A *Newsweek* reviewer of "The Wisdom of Faith with Huston Smith" trivialized Smith as a "spiritual surfer," just as his more academic critics have mistakenly accused him of "eclecticism" and "syncretism." See Rabbi Zalman Schacter-Shalomi & Huston Smith, "Spirituality in Education: A Dialogue," in Steven Glazer (ed), *The Heart of Learning*, 1999, 228, and Nasr, "Homage to Huston Smith," 7.

13 H. Smith, *Tales of Wonder*, xx.

14 Ibid., 41.

15 H. Smith, *The World's Religions*, 390.

16 Marilyn Gustin, "Tribute to Huston Smith," in *Fragments of Infinity*, 13.

PHILIP SHERRARD

1 Philip Sherrard, *The Rape of Man and Nature*, 1987, 114.

2 On Sherrard and Seferis see Peter Mackridge, "The Physical Meta-physician: George Seferis's Spiritual Relationship with Philip Sher-rard," in *This Dialectic of Blood and Light. George Seferis-Philip Sherrard, an Exchange*, ed. Denise Harvey; www.academia.edu/20346697/The_physical_metaphysician.

3 In the *Temenos Academy Review* archive.

4 Garth Fowden, "Philip Sherrard (1922–1995)," obituary, *Anglo-Hellenic Review* 12, 1995.

5 Julie du Boulay in *The Guardian*, June 8, 1995.

6 The book was first published as *The Rape of Man and Nature*, Colombo: Sri Lanka Institute of Traditional Studies, 1987.

7 https://deniseharveypublisher.gr/people/philip-sherrard.

8 Quoted in Kallistos Ware, Foreword to Philip Sherrard, *Christianity: Lineaments of a Sacred Tradition*, 1998, ix. The opening chapter of *The Wound of Greece* originally appeared in 1964 as the Introduction to an anthology which Sherrard edited, *The Pursuit of Greece* (1964).

9 Much of Kazantzakis' work is imbued with this passion but see especially *Report to Greco*, *Zorba the Greek*, *Christ Recrucified*, and *Travels in Greece*.

10 Gary Cyril Jenkins, "The Articulation of the Cosmos," https://lux-christi.wordpress.com/2012/06/12/the-articulation-of-the-cosmos. Lossky was a Russian theologian who spent most of his adult life in exile in Paris. His best known work *is The Mystical Theology of the Eastern Church*, first published in 1944 but appearing in English translation in 1957.

11 Kallistos Ware, Foreword to *Christianity: Lineaments of a Sacred Tradition*, ix.

12 For instance, see Andrew Louth, "The Theology of Creation in Orthodoxy," *International Journal of Orthodox Theology* 8:3 (2017). Louth explores the controversy in which Sherrard crossed swords with Dr John Zizioulas.

13 https://www.temenosacademy.org/?s=Philip+Sherrard. James L. Kelley has accused Sherrard of "dangerous speculations" and "prob-lematic" theological formulations. See James L. Kelley, *Philip Sherrard: Orthodox Theosophy and the Reign of Quantity*, 2015.

14 Temenos Academy website ("Temenos": sacred precinct).

15 See Philip Sherrard, "Kathleen Raine and the Symbolic Imagina-

tion," *Temenos Academy Review* 11, 2008, 180–208. See also Jack Herbert, "Philip Sherrard on "Kathleen Raine and The Symbolic Art:
Some Reactions and Thoughts," *Temenos Academy Review* 12, 2009,
238–47. Sherrard's article also makes clear some divergences in his
and Raine's understanding of and attitude to the perennialist school
of Guénon et al.

16 Kathleen Raine, *Philip Sherrard: A Tribute*, 1996. (This 20-page piece
was available on Amazon for no more than $102 but is now appar-
ently out of print.) On Kathleen Raine's role in The Temenos Academy see Brian Keeble, "Kathleen Raine (1908–2003)," *Sacred Web* 12;
http://www.sacredweb.com/online_articles/sw12_keeble.html.

17 *The Marble Threshing Floor*, quoted by Ware, xxi.

18 Sherrard, *Christianity: Lineaments*, 76–77.

19 See, for example, Sherrard's essay "Christianity and the Metaphysics
of Logic," in *Christianity: Lineaments of a Sacred Tradition*.

20 Ware, xix.

21 James L. Kelley, *Orthodox Theosophy* (italics mine).

22 Lord Northbourne, *Religion in the Modern World*, 1963, 13.

23 S. H. Nasr, "Reflections on Islam and Modern Thought," *The Islamic
Quarterly* XXIII:iii, 1979; 119–31.

24 "Human Image, World Image: The Renewal of Sacred Cosmology,"
in *Towards an Ecology of Transfiguration*, ed. John Chryssavgis &
Bruce V. Flotz, 2013, 216.

25 Sherrard, *Christianity: Lineaments*, 19.

26 Sherrard, *The Rape of Nature*, https://www.themathesontrust.org/
library/the-rape-of-nature.

27 Ruysbroeck quoted in Sherrard, *Christianity: Lineaments*, 208.

MARTIN LUTHER KING JR

1 From *Rediscovering Lost Values*. Many of King's speeches and sermons can be accessed at: https://crossculturalsolidarity.com/mlk-
speeches-sermons-essays/. And at: https://kinginstitute.stanford.edu/
king-papers/documents.

2 *Why Jesus Called a Man a Fool*, August 1967.

3 Wikipedia entry "Martin Luther King."

4 Letter from Birmingham Jail, April 1963.

5 *A Testament of Hope*.

6 *Suffering and Faith*, 1960.

7   Where do we go from here? 11th Annual SCLC Convention, Atlanta, Georgia, August 16, 1967.
8   For a brief discussion of Gandhi's philosophy of nonviolence and ahimsa see "Gandhi, the Cow and the 'Dumb Creation'" in Brian Coman & Harry Oldmeadow, *The Realm of Splendour*, 2021. For some of King's reflections about Gandhi see "My Trip to the Land of Gandhi," *Ebony Magazine*, 1959; https://kinginstitute.stanford.edu/king-papers/documents/my-trip-land-gandhi.
9   There is some dispute as to whether this widely-cited quote actually came from King.
10 *Strength to Love*, 1963.
11 Wikipedia.
12 *The Advocate* (Baton Rouge), April 4, 2018; https://www.theadvocate.com/baton_rouge/opinion/our_views/article_.
13 *Where do we go from here?*, Atlanta, 1967.
14 *A Testament of Hope.*
15 https://mlk.wsu.edu/about-dr-king/famous-quotes/.
16 *Letter from Birmingham Jail.*
17 *Why We Can't Wait*, 1963.
18 Nobel Peace Prize Acceptance Speech, December 1964.
19 *Remaining Awake through a Great Revolution*, March 1968.
20 *Where do we go from here?*
21 Ibid.

JAMES COWAN

1   James Cowan, *The Book with No Name*, 2019.
2   This appeared on James' website which, unhappily, has now been dismantled.
3   The biographical sketch that follows is indebted to the eloquent obituary written by our mutual friend Peter Thompson, *Sydney Morning Herald*, October 30, 2018. Some biographical information can be found in the Wikipedia entry "James Cowan". There is also a good deal of biographical information scattered through his books, the most autobiographical of which is *Two Men Dreaming: A Memoir, A Journey* (1995).
4   *The Book of Letters*, 2018 (unpublished), 35.
5   The anthology was *The Betrayal of Tradition* (2005) which included "Towards a New Dreaming" from *Mysteries of the Dream-Time* (1989).

6 *The Book of Letters*, 35.

7 Peter Mathews, "The Transnational Fantasy: the Case of James Cowan," *Antipodes* 26, June 2012, 68.

8 *The Book of Letters*, as far as I know, remains unpublished. The last work published during James's lifetime was *Palace of Memory: The Secret to King Roger of Sicily's Pleasure Garden*, 2018. We have since seen the appearance of *The Book with No Name*, 2019—on the St. Gallen manuscript, the *Evangelicum Longum*, from circa 900.

9 I later regretted my failure to ask James if he knew Sherrard. I don't recall him ever mentioning him, but James had many connections with people associated with the Temenos Academy, especially Kathleen Raine. It is quite likely that he might have met Sherrard.

10 Interview, innerexplorations.com/chtheomortext/cowan.htm

11 *A Spanner in the Works*, cover blurb.

12 Peter Mathews, "The Transnational Fantasy," 72.

13 For some discussion of the literature on Aboriginal tradition from a perennialist vantage-point see my article, "'Melodies from the Beyond': The Spiritual Traditions of the Australian Aborigines," in *Touchstones of the Spirit: Essays on Religion, Tradition and Modernity*, 2012.

14 The Cowan quotes in the preceding paragraph come from *Mysteries of the Dreamtime*, *The Aborigine Tradition*, and personal correspondence.

15 Bill Neidjie (c.1913–2002), also known as "Kakadu Man," was the last surviving member of his tribe, instrumental in the establishment of the Kakadu National Park, and a respected informant on the old ways.

16 Some of this literature is discussed in my *Black Elk, Lakota Visionary*, 2018.

17 See two articles by Mitchell Rolls: "James Cowan and the white quest for the black self," *Australian Aboriginal Studies*, March 2001, and "The Green Thumb of Appropriation," in *The Littoral Zone: Australian Contexts and their Writers*, ed. C.A. Cranston and Robert Zeller, 2007. See also Peter Mathews, "The Transnational Fantasy." Mathews presents an even-handed discussion of both Cowan's work and Rolls's critique. Mathews' article is a welcome addition to the scanty critical work on Cowan. It includes many valuable insights such as this: "The second phase of Cowan's career [post-1995] presents an implicit challenge to his earlier critics by emphasizing that the real object of his writing lies

not in colonizing any particular cultural tradition, but in reviving the
existential vitality of humanity as a whole." 69.

MARILYNNE ROBINSON

1 *Time*; https://time.com/4298233/marilynne-robinson-2016-time-100/.
2 Ann Patchett, "Whispered in Your Ear: A Moral Man's Good Word,"
   The New York Observer, December 12, 2004.
3 These come from *Gilead*, "Psalm Eight" in *The Death of Adam, When
   I was a child I read books* and *Housekeeping*. Undocumented quotations in the rest of this essay come from *Gilead*.
4 Mark O'Connell, "The First Church of Marilynne Robinson," *The
   New Yorker*, May 30, 2012.
5 Wendell Berry, "The Specialization of Poetry," in *Standing by Words*.
6 See especially "Puritans and Prigs" in *The Death of Adam*.
7 Roger Kimball, "John Calvin Got a Bad Rap," *The New York Times*,
   February 7, 1999
8 Frithjof Schuon, *Spiritual Perspectives and Human Facts*, 1969, 173.
9 From *When I was a child I read books*.
10 Karen Armstrong in *The Guardian*, quoted on the cover of *Absence of
   Mind: The Dispelling of Inwardness from the Modern Myth of the Self*,
   2010. Armstrong's own approach to theology has some affinities with
   Robinson's, as we see in a declaration such as "Theology should be
   like poetry, which takes us to the end of what words and thoughts
   can do." (Cf. Thomas Berry: "Religion is poetry or it is nothing!").
11 Thomas Merton, *No Man is an Island*, 2005, 37.

ALEXANDER ISAYEVICH SOLZHENITSYN

1 *Cancer Ward*.
2 The key works are Camus' *The Plague* (1947) and Böll's *Billiards at
   Half-Past Nine* (1959).
3 Vladimir Solovyov, *Russia and the Universal Church*, 1948, 10; quoted
   in the Wikipedia entry for Solovyov.
4 *One Word of Truth*, Solzhenitsyn's Nobel Prize for Literature acceptance speech which, for various reasons (mainly political, recounted
   in Solzhenitsyn's *The Oak and the Calf*), was never actually delivered
   but sent in text form to the Swedish Academy. It appeared in published form in 1972. Following his exile from the Soviet Union,
   Solzhenitsyn was able to visit Stockholm and receive the Nobel insig-
   nia in 1974.

5 *The Gulag Archipelago.*
6 I think this was in *Winter Notes on Summer Impressions*—but I can't locate it.
7 *A World Split Apart*, Harvard Commencement Address, June, 8, 1978.
8 Distressingly, Solzhenitsyn in his last years became a supporter of Vladimir Putin. There have been various allegations about Solzhenitsyn's fascistic leanings and his purported anti-Semitism. In many instances his utterances have been wrenched out of context and misconstrued. As Solzhenitsyn himself observed, "I would hope that all that has been said about me, slandered about me, in the course of decades, would, like mud, dry up and fall off. It is amazing how much gibberish has been talked about me, more so in the west than in the USSR. In the USSR it was all one-directional propaganda, and (laughs) everyone knew that it was just Communist propaganda," Joseph Pearce, "An Interview with Alexander Solzhenitsyn"; 2003. https://www.catholiceducation.org/en/culture/art/an-interview-with-alexander_-solzhenitsyn.html.
9 *A World Split Apart.*
10 *One Word of Truth.*
11 *A World Split Apart.*
12 *The Gulag Archipelago.*
13 *Men have forgotten God*, The Templeton Prize Acceptance Address, May 10, 1983.
14 *Rebuilding Russia: Reflections and Tentative Proposals.*
15 *Cancer Ward.*
16 *Men have forgotten God.*
17 *A World Split Apart.*
18 Joseph Pearce, "An Interview with Alexander Solzhenitsyn."
19 *Warning to the West* (1976) is a compilation of five speeches given in the USA and Britain in 1975–1976.
20 Prayer quoted in Brian Coman, "'One Word of Truth Shall Outweigh the Whole World': Aleksandr Isayevich Solzhenitsyn 1918–2008," *Quadrant*, September 2008.

Other Books by Harry Oldmeadow

Traditionalism: Religion in the light of Perennial Philosophy, Colombo: Sri Lanka Institute of Traditional Studies, 2000 (Persian translation, 2010. Second Edition, San Rafael, CA: Sophia Perennis, 2011).

Journeys East: 20th-Century Western Encounters with Eastern Religious Traditions, Bloomington: World Wisdom Books, 2004 (French edition Vers l'Orient, Hozhoni, 2018).

A Christian Pilgrim in India: The Spiritual Journey of Swami Abhishiktananda, Bloomington: World Wisdom, 2008 (French edition, 2010).

Mediations: Essays on Religious Pluralism and the Perennial Philosophy, San Rafael, CA: Sophia Perennis, 2008.

Frithjof Schuon and the Perennial Philosophy, Bloomington: World Wisdom, 2010.

Touchstones of the Spirit: Religion, Tradition & Modernity, Bloomington: World Wisdom, 2012.

Black Elk, Lakota Visionary: the Oglala Holy Man and Sioux Tradition, Bloomington: World Wisdom, 2018 (French edition: *Black Elk et l'héritage de la tradition lakota*, Hozhoni, 2020).

Wellsprings (an anthology of maxims and aphorisms), Bendigo: 2019. Reprinted by Carbarita Press, 2021.

Timeless Truths and Modern Delusions: The Perennial Philosophy as a guide for contemporary Buddhists, Melbourne: Platform Books, 2021.

Leaves in the Wind: Memories, Ruminations, Intimations (a memoir), Bendigo: privately printed, 2021.

Gleanings: A Miscellany, Bendigo: Carbarita Press, 2021.

Co-authored with Brian Coman

The Realm of Splendour: Sketches, Reflections and Commentaries on the Natural Order, Bendigo: Carbarita Press, 2021.

Along the Coliban: a journey through landscape and time (Text Brian Coman, Photographs Harry Oldmeadow), Bendigo: Carbarita Press, 2022.

Anthologies Edited

The Betrayal of Tradition, Bloomington: World Wisdom, 2010.

Light from the East, Bloomington: World Wisdom, 2010.

Crossing Religious Frontiers, Bloomington: World Wisdom, 2010.

The Writings of Frithjof Schuon (World Wisdom Series)

The following volumes in this series of new translations of Frithjof Schuon's books, each now annotated and including Selections from Previously Unpublished Letters.

In the Face of the Absolute, 2014.

To Have a Center, 2015.

Treasures of Buddhism, 2018.

Esoterism as Principle and as Way, 2019.

The Eye of the Heart, 2021.

The Play of Masks, 2024.

HARRY OLDMEADOW was formerly Coordinator of Philosophy and Religious Studies at La Trobe University Bendigo, where he also taught Cinema Studies and Literature. His publications include *Journeys East: 20th-Century Western Encounters with Eastern Religious Traditions* (2004); *Traditionalism: Religion in the Light of Perennial Philosophy* (2010); *Touchstones of the Spirit: Religion, Tradition & Modernity* (2012); and *Black Elk, Lakota Visionary* (2018).

www.ingramcontent.com/pod-product-compliance
Lightning Source LLC
Chambersburg PA
CBHW021144090426
42740CB00008B/924